Sir John Fortescue's
A Collision of Giants

Sir John Fortescue's
A Collision of Giants

The British Army During the War of Austrian
Succession & Seven Years' War in Europe
1740-1763

J. W. Fortescue

LEONAUR

Sir John Fortescue's A Collision of Giants
The British Army During the War of Austrian Succession & Seven Years' War in Europe
1740-1763
by J. W. Fortescue

FIRST EDITION

First published under the title
A History of the British Army Vol 2 (Extract)

Leonaur is an imprint of Oakpast Ltd

Copyright in this form © 2015 Oakpast Ltd

ISBN: 978-1-78282-457-2 (hardcover)
ISBN: 978-1-78282-458-9 (softcover)

http://www.leonaur.com

Publisher's Notes

Contents

CHAPTER 1

The Kindling Flame

As the pivotal decade of the 18th century approached all Europe
had been kindled into a blaze of war. On the 20th of October 1740,
while Cathcart was still impatiently awaiting the fair wind which
should carry him from Spithead, the Emperor Charles the Sixth, of
the Holy Roman Empire of the Hapsburgs, died, leaving his daugh-
ter Maria Theresa sole heiress of his dominions. Her succession had
already been recognised by the powers of Europe through their guar-
antee of the Pragmatic Sanction, but on such guarantees little trust
was to be reposed. The principal rival to the Queen of Hungary was
the Elector of Bavaria, and France, mindful of her old friendship with
Bavaria, was ready enough to wreak her old hostility upon the House
of Austria by upholding him. England and Holland alone, commercial
nations to whom a contract was a thing not lightly to be broken, felt
strongly as to their duty in supporting the young queen.

The various states of Germany were as usual self-seeking and disu-
nited, watching greedily to make what profit they could out of the
helpless House of Hapsburg. Frederick of Prussia, not yet named the
Great, was the first to move. He had but recently come to the throne,
inheriting together with it the most efficient army in Europe, and a
large stock of ready money. Moving, as ever, promptly, swiftly, and silently, he invaded Silesia, and by a signal victory over the Austrians at
Mollwitz, (10th April), called the whole of Europe to arms, (April 1st
to 12th, 1741).

France, with visions not only of acquiring new territory in Germany, but of paying off old scores against England through Hanover, had
begun to weave great schemes even before the fight of Mollwitz. The
most remarkable of living French statesmen, Marshal Belleisle, having
thought out his plans and obtained the royal sanction for them, started

off in March 1741 on a tour of visits to the courts of Europe; his object being to persuade them, first to renounce the Pragmatic Sanction, and secondly to support the candidature of the Elector Charles Albert of Bavaria against that of Maria Theresa's husband, the Grand Duke Francis of Lorraine, for the imperial crown. This done, he seems to have hoped to partition Austria proper between Saxony and Prussia, and to divide all Germany and the Empire into four weak kingdoms, Bavaria, Saxony, Prussia, and Hungary, which by careful fostering of jealousies and quarrels should be kept dependent on France.

Charles Albert of Bavaria, Augustus of Saxony, Frederick of Prussia and the Queen of Spain were gained over by Belleisle with little difficulty; but Hanover, with England at its back, stood out for the Pragmatic Sanction. In England the sympathy with Maria Theresa was strong, and Walpole in the session of 1741 obtained from Parliament a pledge to maintain her succession, a subsidy of three hundred thousand pounds to tide her over financial difficulties, and an acknowledgment of England's obligation to assist her with a force of twelve thousand men. He also attempted to detach Frederick from Belleisle's confederacy, but with conspicuous ill success.

Meanwhile King George went over to Hanover to assemble troops for the support of Maria Theresa; and then France, always ready to strike the first blow, sent two armies across the Rhine, one to join hands with the forces of Bavaria and carry the war to the gates of Vienna, the other straight upon Hanover itself. Thus surprised, the king could do nothing but stipulate for one year's neutrality for Hanover, promising also that during the same period he would neither give help to the Queen of Hungary nor cast his vote as an Elector of the Empire in her husband's favour. Bound by this humiliating agreement, which had excited no less scorn in England than in Austria, the king returned home, (Dec. 4th-15th), to meet a new parliament, which had been elected amid no ordinary excitement owing to disasters on the Spanish Main.

Furious attacks were made upon Walpole, who was held responsible for a war which he had always deprecated, and for which he knew the nation to be unprepared; and in less than two months he was driven from office. Lord Wilmington succeeded him, (February, 1742), as nominal head of the Treasury, and Lord Carteret, one of the few living Englishmen who could speak German, took charge of foreign affairs. Parliament showed itself more zealous than ever in the cause of Maria Theresa, and voted her a subsidy of half a million, while

Carteret prevailed with his colleagues to send sixteen thousand British troops to Flanders to act as her auxiliaries in arms. Finally, five millions were granted for the prosecution of the war.

Notwithstanding that all these preparations could be aimed at no power but France, the two nations were not supposed to be at war with each other. The French had invented the phrase *auxiliaries*, and had marched their armies into Germany under the shelter of that innocent designation; and the English were foolish enough for a time to follow their example. The movements of the French fleet at the outset of Wentworth's expedition had, however, left little doubt as to the hostility of France towards England, and the fact had been settled beyond all dispute by some French despatches intercepted by Vernon. The past year therefore had not passed without additional military preparations on the part of England.

In January 1741 four more regiments of marines were raised over and above those sent out with Wentworth; and simultaneously orders were issued for the formation of seven new regiments of foot under Colonels Fowke, Long, Houghton, Price, Cholmondeley, and De Grangue. Of these the first six still remain with us, numbered the Forty-Third to the Forty-Eighth. Throughout the summer also a force of some five thousand men had been kept in camp near Colchester under General Wade, in readiness to take the field. Finally, the estimates for 1742 provided for a force on the British establishment of sixty-two thousand men. Sufficient troops being therefore presumably to hand, the next thing was to appoint a commander, and the choice fell on John, Earl of Stair.

Stair was now close on seventy years of age, but despite a very early beginning of a soldier's life, was still active and efficient enough. At the age of nineteen he had fought at Steenkirk, already with the rank of colonel; in Marlborough's first campaign he had been the foremost in the breach in Cutts's mad assault upon Venloo; he had served as a regimental officer at Blenheim, as a brigadier at Ramillies, on Marlborough's staff at Oudenarde, and had been present also at Malplaquet. He had been distinguished by particular kindness and attention both from the great duke and from Prince Eugene, and had not failed to take to heart their teaching in the art of war. Altogether he was not ill-qualified to command a British army in its first active service on the continent since the death of Marlborough.

His first duties, however, were diplomatic, namely to induce the States-General to permit the occupation of Nieuport and Ostend by the British, as their bases of operations against the French in the Austrian Netherlands. He was further instructed to allay any feeling of distrust that might have been roused by Hanover's declaration of neutrality, and if possible to engage the Dutch to take an active part as auxiliaries of Queen Maria Theresa. It was no easy task, for endless faction joined to an impossible form of government had reduced the Dutch to the lethargy, inefficiency, and helplessness which was their ruin; while, moreover, recollections of the Peace of Utrecht were still strong enough to make them diffident and cold towards any overtures from England.

The proposal to quarter a British garrison in the Netherlands was therefore ill-received, until, in the nick of time, there came the news that the Austrians, having made a desperate push to expel Frederick of Prussia from Silesia, (May 6th-17th), had been totally defeated by him at the Battle of Chotusitz, (May 17). Such a blow to the Austrian cause might bring about great results. Marshal Maillebois, with a French army of forty thousand men, lay in Westphalia, blocking the march of the Hanoverian troops if they should try to join the British, and at the same time ready to pierce into Holland at any moment. In such circumstances a contingent of British troops could not but be valuable to the States, so leave was granted for the disembarkation of the first British battalions at Ostend; and arrangements were made, though with no very good grace, to find them quarters in Bruges and Ghent. But as to throwing in their lot with the British for the defence of the Pragmatic Sanction, the machinery of the Dutch Government was too complicated, the minds of men too cautious, and the spirit of those in authority too corrupt, to permit the settlement of a matter of such importance without delay of months or even years.

The British troops continued to arrive in driblets from England, and Stair meanwhile, knowing that his movements must depend upon those of the French, watched the situation with the keenest interest. The French army of Bavaria, after a few trifling successes on the Danube, had been rapidly swept back by the energy of the Austrian General Khevenhüller. A portion of it, which had penetrated into Bohemia and captured Prague, was still lying in that kingdom under an incompetent commander, Marshal Broglie, with Prague for its base. Little was to be feared from Broglie: the really formidable enemy was Frederick of Prussia, whom Stair was for detaching from Belleisle's confederacy at any cost.

The Prussian Army once out of the way, the whole armed force of Austria could be turned upon the French in Bohemia, who, owing to Khevenhüller's successes on the Danube, must either be sacrificed altogether, or rescued with great difficulty at the price of denuding the whole French frontier of troops. It would then be open to the Austrians to advance through the Palatinate and up the Moselle into France, while the Dutch and English might either join them or break straight in from the north upon Paris and put an end to the war and to the mischief of French ambition for ever.

So counselled Stair, with a clearness of judgment, alike as soldier and statesman, that was not unworthy of his great master; but unfortunately Maria Theresa would not come to terms with Frederick without striking a last blow for Silesia, which ended, as has been told, in the disaster of Chotusitz. Then at last she gave in; and the Treaty of Breslau, (June 11th), purchased the friendship of Frederick at the cost of Silesia. Stair was instantly on the alert, for the game seemed now to be in his hand. The French frontier towards the Netherlands was but weakly defended; a feint of invasion in that direction must certainly bring back Maillebois from Westphalia to guard it, and then the road would be open for the junction of the Hanoverians with the British. The Austrians had already fourteen thousand troops in the country, which, added to the British and their Allies, would make up a force superior to any that Maillebois could bring together.

Carteret entered warmly into the plan; and meanwhile events elsewhere had fallen out exactly according to Stair's prevision. The Austrians, relieved from the pressure of Frederick and his Prussians, turned all their strength against the French in Bohemia, and swept them out of all their posts except Prague, wherein they held the wreck of the French force closely besieged.

Maillebois was called away to Bohemia to save the beleaguered army if he could, and the whole of the French frontier towards Flanders lay open, with little more than twenty thousand men to protect it. This was the moment for which Stair had waited, hardly daring to hope that it would ever come, and he urged that the whole of the forces present, alike of England, Hanover, and Austria, should be concentrated for an immediate attack on Dunkirk, where the best of the French troops were known to be gathered together. These troops once beaten, the road would be clear for a march to Paris.

But just at this moment King George suddenly turned lukewarm. He was not at war with France, he said, and his troops were acting simply as auxiliaries to the Queen of Hungary. France could take no offence at their presence, as her troops were likewise employed only as auxiliaries to the Elector of Bavaria. Again, there were sundry arrangements to be adjusted before the troops of the Allies could be concentrated. It was, therefore, not until the 24th of August that orders were despatched to the Hanoverians to march; and even then King George was inclined rather to bar the return march of Maillebois from Bohemia at the Meuse than to strike at the heart of his enemy at Dunkirk. Then, again, the men of skill in England, as Stair contemptuously called the council of war at Whitehall, thought the attack on Dunkirk too venturesome; and the plan was disapproved, chiefly, it should seem, because the king had some idea of taking command of the army in person.

Stair meanwhile was chafing with impatience, concerting new plans with the Austrian commanders, and promising himself that his winter quarters should be in Normandy. His design now was to march straight for the head of the Oise, which would give him a navigable river for his transport, and to move from thence direct upon Paris. The French troops on the spot were few in number and would not dare to leave Dunkirk. The road for two-thirds of the journey to the Oise was paved, and the short distance that remained, therefore, constituted the only difficulty, by no means insuperable, in the way. Arrived at Paris the army could take artillery from the arsenal there, and move down the Seine to the siege of Havre. Finally, Stair promised that, if the king would give him a free hand, he would enable him before the 12th of October to dictate his own terms.

The plan was daring enough, but Stair was neither a visionary nor an idle boaster, and there appears no reason to doubt that it was perfectly feasible. The French had recently fortified Dunkirk anew, and, as was not uncommon with them, had elaborated the works to such excess that forty thousand men were required to defend them. Unless, therefore, they chose to abandon Dunkirk, which they could hardly afford to do, there remained no troops to check an advance on Paris. But the design did not commend itself to the king. He submitted it to General Wade, slowest and most cautious of generals, who criticised it adversely; and meanwhile, whether through jealousy or treachery or sheer mismanagement, the orders for the Hanoverians to march were on one pretext or another delayed until all hopes of a campaign of 1742 were banished by the coming of the winter.

Stair was deeply chagrined; and the discipline of his troops, who had been long kept idle in quarters which they detested, suffered so much that it was only restored by the strongest measures. The winter set in with unusual severity, making the ground easy for purposes of transport and neutralising the value of the inundations on which the fortresses of the north-west frontier of France depended chiefly for their defence. Stair was eager to pounce upon some of them while the frost lasted, but the Austrian generals would not hear of it. He then proposed to attack one or other of the fortresses in Lorraine, Metz, Longwy, or Thionville, preparatory to an invasion of France by the Moselle; but again the Austrians dissented. Their great object was to move King George's army into Germany, in order to frighten some of the minor German princes into alliance with Austria; and Stair, as he bitterly complained, was so much hampered by his instructions that he felt absolutely helpless. The Hanoverians again, though supposed to be under his command, received independent orders from the king which were not communicated to Stair, and they declined to obey any other.

At last, after many struggles with Austrian generals and English ministers, the British Army in February 1743 began its march eastward, as the February. Austrians had desired. The regiments were sadly distressed by the absence of multitudes of officers, who had gone home on leave for their duties in Parliament or for more private and trivial objects Stair wrote with biting sarcasm:

> I thought it hard to refuse them leave when they said that their preferment depended on the interest of their friends at Court. They had no notion that it depended on their exertions here.

To such a pass had twenty years of peace under Walpole brought the discipline of the army.

Nevertheless Stair's recent severity had borne good fruit, and the conduct both of officers and men in a winter's march of extreme hardship and discomfort was such as to call forth his warmest praise.[1] As the spring drew near, the question as to the plan of the coming campaign became urgent. Fifty thousand French troops had been moved to the Moselle to bar any invasion through Lorraine, while all their forces in Flanders had been stationed on the Meuse ready either to join their comrades on the Moselle, or to advance to the Neckar in case the Allies should cross the Rhine to the south of Cologne. Stair, with the spirit of his master strong upon him, hinted at the desirability

---

1. The Guards set the example.

13

of a march to the Danube. The Austrians, as he guessed, would certainly resume their advance from the east against the French on that river as soon as the weather permitted, and his plan was to close in upon them from the west and fall upon their rear while the Austrians attacked them in front.

Such a project, however, was too bold for the caution of King George, and, moreover, as he was always reminding Stair, though the French were to be treated as enemies he was not at war with France. His final orders, given after immense delay, were that Stair should occupy the heights of Mainz and command the junction of the Rhine and Main. Such a disposition was from a military point of view sufficiently obscure; and indeed it had no military object whatever, being designed simply to secure the choice of King George's nominee for the vacant electorate of Mainz.

Very slowly, owing to the extreme difficulty of obtaining forage, the forces, both native and mercenary, of England, Hanover, and Austria were assembled on the north bank of the Main. Their position extended from the Rhine to Aschaffenburg, and faced to the south, while a bridge of boats was kept ready at Frankfort for the passage of the river. Meanwhile, a French Army of seventy thousand men, under Marshal Noailles, had quietly taken up its station on the Upper Rhine near Spires, and was seeking to establish communication with Bavaria and the Neckar, in order to save what was left of Broglie's army while still it might; though, at the same time, not without apprehensions as to the danger of leaving the Palatinate and Lorraine open behind it.

Stair took in the situation at a glance. He was for crossing the Main, following the left bank downward and taking up a position between Oppenheim and Mainz. There he could threaten Noailles so closely that he would not dare to detach any part of his army to Bavaria. He would, moreover, have it in his power to attack the French on the Neckar whenever he pleased; and finally, he could in due time cross the Rhine westward, and force the French to retire on Landau and Alsace, leaving Lorraine and the Netherlands open to invasion.

After some trouble Count d'Arenberg, a general neither very enterprising nor very capable, who commanded the Austrians, appears to have been converted to his views; and though the entire army was even now not yet arrived at the rendezvous, the Allies on the 3rd of June began the passage of the Main. A day or two later Stair received intelligence that Noailles had left the Neckar and was advancing along the high road from Darmstadt to Frankfort to attack him. This road passed for a considerable distance through a forest, and it was at its outlet from this forest that Stair took up his position to await the French. D'Arenberg so strongly disapproved of the whole proceeding that he withdrew the whole of the Austrian dragoons to the right bank of the Main, in order to rescue the shattered remnants that should be left of Stair's army after the battle. Marshal Neipperg, his second, however, led the Austrian infantry to the position of Stair's choice: and when Noailles arrived on the following morning he withdrew without venturing to attack.

Meanwhile King George, who had arrived at Hanover a fortnight before, was perfectly frantic. On Stair's first proposal to cross to the south bank of the Main he had sent positive orders, which reached Stair too late, that he was not to stir. The king was surrounded by nervous Austrians who, having information of Noailles's intended advance, were, or professed to be, in terror lest the Allies should be beaten in detail, and did not fail to represent how dreadful it would be if the army should be defeated before His Majesty could take command. Letter after letter therefore was despatched to Stair, bidding him above all things to be careful, and finally ordering him to repass the Main. Stair at first had prepared to obey orders, though not without speaking his mind, he wrote:

> I am too careful of the king's interest to be rash, but I am sure of two things, that the French are far more occupied with Bavaria than with us, and that we are superior to them even in numbers. The importance of giving an army to a person who is trusted is now evident. Had my plan been followed, we should now be in a position to fall on the head of the French army which, after sending away a detachment to Bavaria, is now taking post along the Rhine.

In truth, during the months of May and June, the Austrians on the Danube had swept Broglie right out of Germany; and Noailles's detachment no sooner reached him than it was ordered forthwith to retreat. But when Stair heard of Noailles's advance to attack him he quietly suppressed the king's orders to repass the Main until he had offered battle to the French. When Noailles refused it, Stair recrossed the river as he had been bidden, unwillingly indeed, yet not a little satisfied that after all the king's orders and all the Austrian predictions of disaster, he had successfully proved the soundness of his views. "But," he added significantly on arriving on the northern bank, "it will be impossible for us now to find forage. The French being masters of one side of the river, forage cannot be brought down to us by water, so we must move upward." It was just this question of supplies which had made him so anxious for a general action; and the event proved that he was right.[2]

---

2. I have entered into some detail over Stair's part in the campaign, since he is charged, even by Lord Mahon, with the responsibility for the situation of the army just before Dettingen. "Lord Stair, whose military genius, never very bright, was rusted with age, appears to have committed blunder on blunder." Vol. iii.

Chapter 2

Dettingen

On the 19th of June King George at last arrived from Hanover and took over the command of the army, which was encamped, as he had ordered, on the right bank of the Main, the English and Hanoverians lying about Aschaffenburg. In the hope of securing forage on the other bank, a battery had been erected on the bridge of Aschaffenburg, but Noailles, moving up to the river, erected a redoubt at his own end of the bridge and put an end to all such hopes. Meanwhile he seized a post further up the river to intercept all supplies from Franconia, and threw two bridges over it below Aschaffenburg at Seligenstadt, by which his troops could cross and cut off the Allies from their magazines at Hanau. For a week the king remained helpless in this camp, unwilling to retreat though his peril increased every day. The result was that he found himself in command of a starving army. It was impossible to keep the soldiers from plunder, and discipline became seriously relaxed. At last, on the 26th of June, it was perforce resolved that the army must retreat to Hanau that very night.

Meanwhile Noailles had not been idle. The ground on which the Allies were encamped is a narrow plain pent in between the Spessart Hills and the Main. These hills are densely wooded, and the forest appears at that time to have descended lower into the plain than at present. When therefore the Allies retired to Hanau, as Noailles knew that inevitably they must, it would be impossible for them to keep out of range of cannon posted on the opposite bank of the Main, and accordingly the marshal had erected five different batteries to play upon them during their march. At one o'clock on the morning of the 27th intelligence was brought to him that the Allies were in motion. This was the moment for which he had been waiting.

Instantly galloping to Seligenstadt, he ordered Count Grammont

17

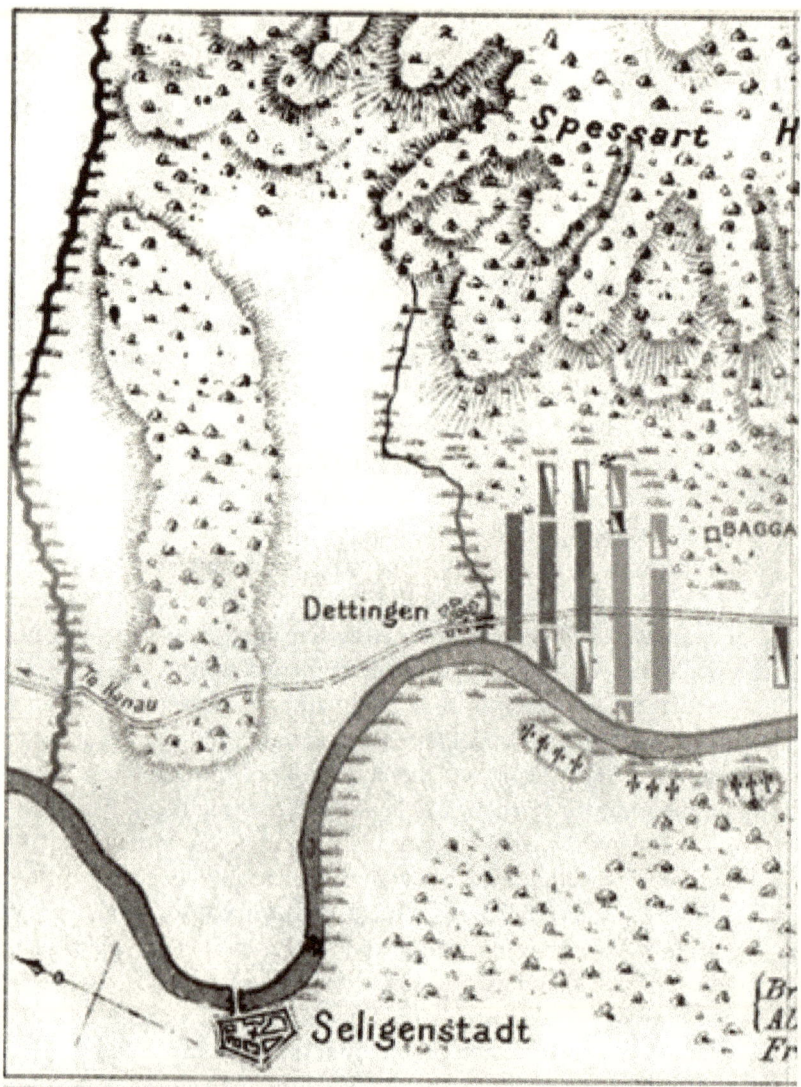

Spessart H

BAGGA

Dettingen

To Hanau

Seligenstadt

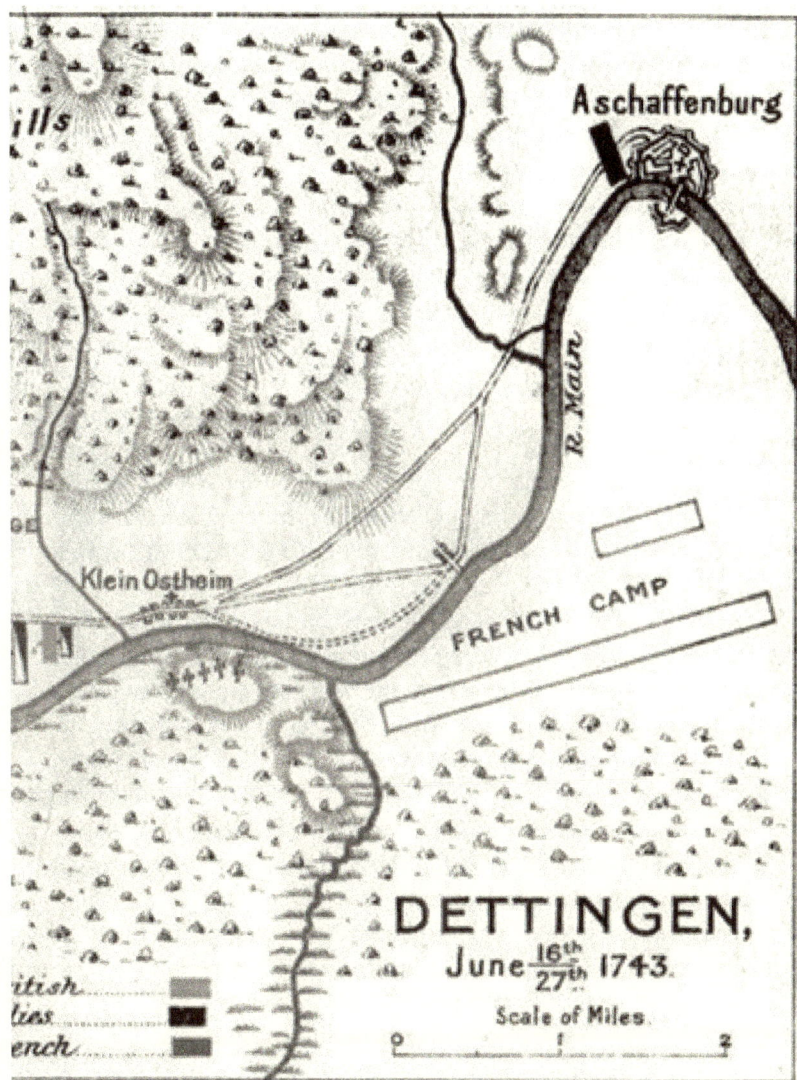

Aschaffenburg

R. Main

Klein Ostheim

FRENCH CAMP

DETTINGEN,
June $\frac{16th}{27th}$ 1743.

Scale of Miles

0   1   2

itish
lies
ench

to cross the Main with twenty-eight thousand men by the two bridges which he had laid for the purpose, and to take up a position about a mile up the river by the village of Dettingen. At that point a rivulet runs down across the plain from the Spessart Hills to the Main, through a little boggy dale which was uncrossed by any bridge except by that of the high road to Hanau. There Grammont was bidden to wait and to make an end of the Allies as they defiled over the bridge. He took up his position accordingly, and Noailles returned to the opposite bank of the Main to direct his operations against King George's flank and rear.

It was four o'clock in the morning before the Allied Army was fairly in motion. The British cavalry led the way, followed by the Austrian, then came the British infantry and the Austrian infantry after them; and last of all came a strong rear-guard composed of the British Guards, the choicest of the German infantry, and the Hanoverian cavalry; for it was in the rear that an attack of the French was most looked for and most to be dreaded. The apprehensions of a French advance on Aschaffenburg were soon seen to be well founded. The march of the Allies from that town lay across a bend of the Main to the village of Klein Ostheim, and as they approached the river they could see the French on the opposite bank in full march to cross the river behind them and cut off their retreat up the stream.

Thus Noailles's dispositions were complete. These troops were to block the Allies to the south, impenetrable woods shut them off from the east, the Main barred their way on the west, and Grammont stood before them at Dettingen on the north. Noailles had caught them, as he said, in a mouse-trap, and might reasonably feel certain that they could not escape.

On arriving about seven o'clock at Klein Ostheim, the whole army of the Allies was obliged to file through it by a single road. The cavalry, therefore, when it had passed through the village was halted and wheeled round with its face to the river to wait till the infantry should come up. This again Noailles had foreseen, and he had planted his cannon in exactly the right place to play upon the Allies when they should advance beyond the village. For an hour the cavalry stood halted before the march could be resumed; and now came intelligence from an advanced party in Dettingen that Grammont was in order of battle in front and that an immediate engagement was inevitable. King George hastened to set his army likewise in order of battle; but all the baggage had been massed between the first and second divisions

BATTLE OF DETTINGEN

of the column of route, and the confusion for a time was very great. Meanwhile the French troops bound for Aschaffenburg had by this time cleared the front of the first of Noailles' s batteries and left the guns free to open fire. The shot soon came humming thick and fast into the heavy mass of waggons and baggage-animals, and the confusion increased.

Guns were sent for in frantic haste to silence the French cannon, but the artillery being far in the rear was long in making its appearance: and meanwhile the king capered about on horseback in great excitement, staff-officers galloped to and fro, and the troops marched and counter-marched into their positions, always under the deadly fire of the French battery. Gradually, though with infinite difficulty, the troops were shuffled into their places, for the stereotyped order of battle was useless in a plain that permitted a frontage only of twenty-three battalions and a few squadrons at most. So passed a terrible hour and more, until at last the British guns came into action and replied effectively to the French batteries; and then a push was made to shift the baggage into a place of safety. In the middle of the plain between Klein Ostheim and Dettingen stood a wood flanked on each hand by a morass. Two lines of cavalry were moved forward towards this wood, the baggage followed them, the infantry followed the baggage, and the troublesome waggons were at last stowed away securely under cover of the trees, while the cavalry and the Austrian infantry made haste to form the right of the Allies' line of battle.

It was high time, for it was now almost noon, and Grammont, tired of remaining where he had been bidden to wait on the north side of Dettingen, or believing (as he himself said) that the Allies had already passed him and that only their rear-guard was left, had advanced beyond the ravine to take up a fresh position. So far as the Allies could see, he was manoeuvring to move troops down under cover of the forest upon their right flank. By this time, however, King George's line was formed, and on its extreme left were seen the scarlet coats of the British battalions. To the left of all, and within a furlong of the river, stood the Thirty-third Foot, and to its right in succession the Twenty-First Fusiliers, Twenty-Third Fusiliers, Twelfth, Eleventh, Eighth and Thirteenth Foot.

On the right of the Thirteenth stood an Austrian brigade, and then in succession the Blues, Life Guards, Sixth Dragoons, and Royal Dragoons. All of these were in the first line. In the second line, in rear of their comrades on the left, were posted the Twentieth, Thirty-Second,

KING GEORGE AT THE BATTLE OF DETTINGEN

Thirty-Seventh, Thirty-First, and the Buffs; and in rear of the cavalry on the right, the Seventh Dragoon Guards, King's Dragoon Guards, Fourth and Seventh Dragoons, and the Scots Greys.

Opposite to them the French were ranged in two lines with a reserve in third line, the infantry being in the centre and the cavalry on the flanks, so that the famous French Household Cavalry,[1] in its place of honour on the extreme right, stood opposed to the British battalions on the Allied left. General Clayton, who commanded on the left, observing the mass of cavalry that confronted him, sent hastily for the Third Dragoons to fill up the gap between the Thirty-third and the river, and therewith the British dispositions were complete.

The whole of the first line then advanced, the king, who had with difficulty been prevented from stationing himself on the extreme left, waving his sword and shouting words of encouragement with a broad German accent. Fortunately the French were themselves in great disorder and confusion. The corrupt dealing in the appointment and promotion of officers, which fifty years later was to set the French army on the side of the Revolution, was already undermining efficiency and discipline. Grammont on advancing beyond the ravine had thought out no new order of a battle. Not a brigadier was competent to draw up his brigade, and the Household Cavalry kept manoeuvring about in front of the infantry without a thought except for the fine figure that it was cutting in the sight of both armies.

The advance of the Allies was necessarily slow, for some of the English regiments, whose way lay through the morasses, were knee-deep in mire. The whole line was presently halted to take breath, and the British, evidently a little shaken by the previous hurry and confusion and by the gesticulations of the king, broke into a feeble and irregular cheer, a sound which Lord Stair heard with great displeasure. The line was dressed and the advance was resumed in better order, though the French batteries on the other bank of the Main never ceased to rain destruction on the Third Dragoons and on the unfortunate battalions on the left.

The men were not yet quite steady, for some undisciplined spirits, fretting at the incessant parade of the French Household Cavalry, opened an irregular fire all along the line. Then, as it seems, came the most comical incident of the day. King George's horse, frightened by the crackle of the musketry, took the bit in his teeth and bolted away to the rear, His Majesty, with purple face and eyes starting out of his

---

3. *Maison du Roi.*

24

head, pulling desperately at him with both hands but unable to stop him. Ultimately the animal's career was checked, and the king returning to the right of the line dismounted and resumed his gestures on foot, utterly fearless, as are all of his race, and confident that his own legs, at least, would carry him in the right direction. The line was again halted to load, there being fortunately still time to repair previous faults, and the advance was again resumed with greater steadiness.

Then the French infantry of the Guard on Grammont's right centre advanced likewise, cheering loudly, and opened a fitful and disorderly fire. The British, now thoroughly in hand, answered with a regular, swift, and continuous fire of platoons, the ranks standing firm like a wall of brass and pouring in volley after volley, deadly and unceasing such a fire as no French officer had ever seen before. [2] The French Guards staggered under it and the British again raised an irregular cheer. "Silence," shouted Stair imperiously, galloping up. "Now one and all together when I give the signal." And as he raised his hat the British broke into the stern and appalling shout which was to become so famous on the fields of the Peninsula. The French Guards waited for no more when they heard it, but shrank back in disorder in rear of their horse, which now advanced in earnest against the extreme British left.

Clayton saw the danger. His left flank in the general confusion had never been properly secured, and though the fire of the French batteries by the river had ceased lest it should destroy their own troops, yet the Third Dragoons and the Thirty-third had been much weakened by it during their advance. Despatching urgent messages for reinforcements of cavalry, he put a bold face on the matter, ordered the dragoons, Thirty-Third, Twenty-First, and Twenty-Third forward to meet the French attack, and prepared to stand the shock. Down came the flower of the French cavalry upon them, sword in hand, at high speed. The Third Dragoons were the first to close with them. They were but two weak squadrons against nine squadrons of the enemy, their depth was but of three ranks against eight ranks of the French; but they went straight at them, burst into the heart of them and cut their way through, though with heavy loss. The Thirty-Third faced the attack as boldly, never gave way for an inch and brought men and horses crashing down by their eternal rolling fire.

Next to them the two regiments of fusiliers were even more hardly pressed. The *gendarmerie* came down upon them at full trot with pistols

2. *Mémoires de Noailles.*

in both hands and swords dangling by the wrist. Arrived within range they fired the pistols, dashed the empty weapons in the faces of the British, and then fell in with the sword; but the fusiliers, as it was said, fought like devils, their platoon-fire thundering out as regularly as on parade, and the French horse fell back repulsed.

Still, gallantly as this first attack had been met, the numerical superiority of the French cavalry was formidable, and there was imminent danger lest the British left flank should be turned. The Third Dragoons had suffered heavily, after their first charge, from the bullets of a battalion posted in support of the French horse, but they rallied, and twice more, weak and weary as they were, they charged ten times their numbers and cut their way through them. But after the third charge they were well-nigh annihilated. All the officers except two, and three-fourths of the men and horses had been killed or wounded; two of the three standards had been cut to atoms, both silk and staves, by shot and shell, and in the last charge the third had dropped from a cornet's wounded hand and lay abandoned on the ground.

A trooper of the regiment, Thomas Brown by name, was just dismounting to recover it when a French sabre came down on his bridle-hand and shore away two of his fingers. His horse, missing the familiar pressure of the bit, at once bolted, and before he could be pulled up had carried his rider into the rear of the French lines. There Dragoon Brown saw the standard of his regiment borne away in triumph by a French *gendarme*. Disabled as he was he rode straight at the Frenchman, attacked and killed him; and then gripping the standard between his leg and the saddle he turned and fought his way single-handed through the ranks of the enemy, emerging at last with three bullet holes through his hat and seven wounds in his face and body, but with the standard safe.

But now the First and Seventh Dragoons, which had been summoned from the right, came galloping up and fell in gallantly enough upon the French Household Cavalry. These were, however, repulsed, partly, it should seem, because they attacked with more impetuosity than order, partly because the French were armed with helmets and breastplates heavy enough to turn a pistol shot. The Blues followed close after them, but sacrificing order to speed were, like their comrades, driven back in confusion; and the French *gendarmes*, flushed with success, bore down for the second time upon the Twenty-First and Twenty-Third and succeeded in breaking into them.

But the two battalions were broken only for a moment. Quickly

King's Own Dragoons at Dettingen

recovering themselves they faced inwards, and closing in upon the French in their midst shot them down by scores. The Fourth and Sixth British Dragoons, together with two regiments of Austrian dragoons, now came up and renewed the combat against the French Household Cavalry, but it was not until after they had been twice repulsed that at last they succeeded, with the help of their rallied comrades, in forcing back the intrepid squadrons of the French horse.

Meanwhile the battle elsewhere had flagged. A feeble attack of the French against the right of the Allies had been easily repelled, and in the centre the second line of the French infantry had cared little more than the first to face the terrible English fire. But while the *gendarmerie* were still pressing the British hard on the left, the French Black Musketeers suddenly broke away from their place by their side, and wheeling to their left galloped madly between the fire of friendly and hostile infantry to make a dash upon the British Royal Dragoons at the extreme right of the Allied line. The Austrian Marshal Neipperg no sooner saw them than he exclaimed: "Now is the time. The British horse will attack in front, and our horse in flank, and the thing is done."

British and Austrians at once closed in upon the Black Musketeers, cut them to pieces, and then bore down upon the flank of the French infantry. The French foot, which had behaved very unworthily of itself all day, now took to its heels and fled in confusion towards the Main. The British horse on the left, one regiment in particular burning to wipe out the humiliation of its first failure, pressed the French Household Cavalry harder than ever in front, and the Scots Greys plunging in upon their flank threw them into utter rout. The whole French army now made headlong for the fords and bridges of the Main, the infantry in their panic plunging madly into the stream and perishing by scores if not by hundreds in the water. Now was the moment for a vigorous pursuit, and had Stair been left to work his own will the French would have suffered very heavily; but the king was too thankful to have escaped from Noailles's mousetrap to think of turning his good fortune to account. The marshal was allowed to retreat in peace, and thus, after four hours of sharp work, ended the Battle of Dettingen.

Seldom has a commander found more fortunate issue from a series of blunders than King George. Had Grammont obeyed his orders it is difficult to see how a man of the Allied Army could have escaped; but even allowing for Grammont's ill-timed impatience it is strange that

Noailles should have allowed the day to go as it went. It is true that he had sent the best of his troops across the Main with Grammont, but he had still from twenty to thirty thousand men on his own side of the river whom he left standing idle, without an attempt to employ them. He seems, in fact, to have been paralysed with dismay over the wreck of his very skilful combinations. The action itself deserves the name of a combat rather than a battle, for on neither side was more than half of the force really engaged; yet Dettingen was decidedly a victory, for the French were badly beaten and lost little, if any, less than five thousand men, killed, wounded, and prisoners. The loss of the Allies was about half of that number, of which the British share was two hundred and sixty-five killed and five hundred and sixty-one wounded, the most valuable life taken being that of General Clayton.

As the brunt of the action fell wholly on the first line, the greatest sufferers among the infantry were the regiments chiefly exposed to the flanking fire of the French batteries. These were the Thirty-Third, Twenty-First, Twenty-Third, and Twelfth of the Line, but in not one of them did the casualties exceed one hundred men, or about an eighth of their strength. The cavalry suffered far more heavily in comparison, though here again the losses of the heroes of the day, the Third Dragoons, were more than twice as great as those of any other regiment: one hundred and fifty men and as many horses forming a terrible proportion of casualties in two squadrons.

The most noticeable points in the engagement were the disgraceful behaviour of the French infantry, by no one more severely censured than by Noailles himself, and the deadly accuracy of the British fire. A smaller but curious fact is that both the king and the Duke of Cumberland were run away with by their horses, the former, as has been told, to the rear, the latter to the front, and indeed into the midst of the French infantry, from which, however, he emerged with no greater hurt than a bullet in the leg. At the close of the day the king was so much elated by his success as to revive the creation of knights banneret in the field, a proceeding which ceases to seem ridiculous when we learn that Lord Stair was the first and Dragoon Thomas Brown the last of the new knights. Such a scene was never to be seen again, for Dettingen was the last action in which a king of England actually commanded his army in person.

The ceremony of knighthood completed, the king left his wounded on the ground to the care of Noailles, and hastened away as quickly as possible with the army to his magazine at Hanau. The battle virtually closed the campaign, so far as the British were concerned, and King George returned home with his laurels fresh upon him, to be hailed with acclamation as a victor, and hear his praises sung in endless *stanzas* of most execrable verse. A few months later Lord Stair also returned home, without recrimination and without complaint, but with resolute and scornful determination to resign the command, since he was not trusted with the conduct of operations. General Wade was appointed field-marshal, (December), to command in his stead. Finally, some weeks later the ridiculous fiction, that the principal combatants were acting only as auxiliaries to rival claimants to the Empire, was abandoned, and open war was declared against France, (March 1744). Had this straightforward course been adopted two years before, Stair would probably have turned the date of the declaration of war into that of the conclusion of an honourable peace. As matters stood the war was prolonged, and the time of its avowed inception was chosen as the moment for discarding the ablest of living British generals.

Our noble generals played their parts,
Our soldiers fought like thunder,
Prince William too, that valiant heart
In fight performed wonders.
Though through the leg with bullet shot
The Prince his wound regarded not,
But still maintained his post and fought
For glorious George of England.

—*Stanza*, broadsheet,
British Museum.

30

CHAPTER 3

The Battle of Fontenoy

However fortunate might be the issue of Dettingen, it served at least its purpose in preventing the despatch of French reinforcements to the Danube and to Bohemia; and the campaign of 1743 closed with the utter collapse of Belleisle's great schemes and with the expulsion of the French from Germany. It was now clear that the war would be carried on in the familiar cockpit of the Austrian Netherlands. Such a theatre was convenient for France, since it lay close to her own borders, and convenient for the Allies, because the Dutch had at last been persuaded to join them, and because the British would be brought nearer to their base at Ostend. Marshal Saxe, whose fine talent had hitherto been wasted under incompetent French Generals in Bohemia, was appointed to the chief command of the French in Flanders; and every effort was made to give him a numerous and well -equipped army, and to enable him to open his campaign in good time.

In England the preparations by no means corresponded with the necessities of the position. The estimates indeed provided for a force of twenty-one thousand British in Flanders in 1744 as against sixteen thousand in the previous year, but only at the cost of depleting the weak garrison left in England; for the actual number of men voted for the two years was the same. All British officers of experience strongly urged upon the government the importance of being first in the field, but when an army was to be made up in different proportions of English, Dutch, Germans, and Austrians it needed a Marlborough to bring the discordant Courts into harmony as well as to make ready the troops for an early campaign.

By the beginning of April eighty thousand French soldiers had marched from their winter quarters, and were concentrated on the frontier between the Scheldt and the Sambre, while the Allies were still scattered about in cantonments, not exceeding even then a total strength of fifty-five thousand men. Wade, the English commander, delayed first by confusion at home and next by contrary winds, was still in England while the French were concentrating, and not a single English recruit to repair the losses of the past campaign had arrived in Flanders. Then arose disputes as to the disposition of the Allied forces, both Austrians and Dutch being nervously apprehensive of leaving their towns on the frontier without garrisons.

When in the second week in May the Allied Army was at last collected close to Brussels, it was still weaker by twenty thousand men than it should have been, and found itself confronted with the task of holding Flanders, Brabant, Hainault, and the Sambre against a superior force of French. May passed away and June came, but the Allies remained helpless and motionless in their camp, while Saxe, after a short march westward, turned north and advanced steadily between the Scheldt and the Lys. His principal object was not very difficult to divine.

By the middle of June his detachments had seized Ypres and Fort Knock, which commanded the canal from Nieuport to Ypres, thus cutting off the British from one of their bases on the coast. It remained to be seen whether he would aim next at Ostend, where the whole of the British stores of ordnance were accumulated, or whether he would attempt Bruges and Ghent in order to secure the navigation of the Bruges Canal as well as of the Scheldt and Lys. Again, it was always open to him, if he pleased, to besiege Tournay, a fortress which the Allies would not willingly lose. Thus the problem set to the Allies was not easy of solution; but of all solutions they chose the worst.

The Dutch and Austrians could not bear the notion of forsaking any one of their darling strongholds, and insisted that the strength of the army should be frittered away in providing weak garrisons for the defence of all. Wade, to do him justice, was for keeping all the troops together, crossing the Scheldt, and taking up a strong position to cover Ghent; but the Austrians would not consent lest they should expose Brussels. Wade was certainly not a strong man, but he must not be too hardly judged. Marlborough had spent the most anxious days of all his campaigns in distraction between the safety of Ghent and of Brussels, and had only extricated himself by the march that preceded the battle of Oudenarde.

Meanwhile King George had been exerting himself with great energy, but two months too late, to provide Wade with additional

BATTLE OF FONTENOY

troops, both British and Dutch, and had begged that Prince Charles of Lorraine might cross the Rhine with his whole army, and direct the operations in Flanders as Commander-in Chief of all the Allies. It was a wise step in every way, since the prince's relationship to Queen Maria Theresa assured to him the seniority in rank which was needed to hold so heterogeneous a host in coherence. Prince Charles did his share of the work admirably, forcing his passage across the Rhine with great skill in the face of the French, and taking up a strong position on the frontier of Alsace. A few days later the British reinforcements reached Wade, and King George issued positive orders to him to take the offensive and "commence hostilities of all kinds."

It seemed, indeed, as if the time were come for pressing home upon the French; but just at this critical moment Frederick of Prussia intervened in favour of France, and by a threat to invade Bohemia brought Prince Charles back quickly over the Rhine. None the less Wade and his fellows held a council of war and resolved to bring Saxe to action if possible. King George gave his gracious approval to their plan, and on the 31st of July the Allies turned westward and crossed the Scheldt. It still remained to be seen, however, whether Saxe would allow an action to be forced on him; for he lay now, entrenched to the teeth, on the Lys between Menin and Courtrai, which was a pretty clear indication that he would not.

At this moment Lord Stair, who had followed the course of operations carefully from England, came forward, like a true pupil of Marlborough, with a new plan of campaign. His advice was that the Allies should turn Saxe's tactics against himself. They should march south to Orchies, between Lille and Tournay, and there encamp, where they would be within reach of half a dozen French fortified towns. The French would not dare to leave the fortresses defenceless; and the garrisons necessary to render them secure would absorb the whole of their force in the field. Then the Allies could send detachments into France and lay Picardy under contribution, or possibly carry out the plan, rejected two years before, of a march to the Seine. The King of Prussia's action only made some bold stroke of the kind the more imperative.

Stair had gained over the Austrian general D'Arenberg to this project in 1742; but it was hardly likely to be accepted by him now. Carteret, in forwarding Stair's memorandum to Wade, gave him no positive orders except at least to do something; but poor Wade found it impossible to make the Austrians do anything. The Allies having crossed the Scheldt halted inactive for weeks, and no persuasion could induce D'Arenberg to move. At last the army did march down to the plains of Lille, but without its artillery, so that it could not be said seriously to threaten the French fortresses. The Dutch and Austrians had undertaken to furnish a siege-train, but had taken no step to procure one of the ten thousand horses that were required to transport it.

After a short sojourn in the south the Allies marched helplessly northward once more. August passed away and September came, but even in the fourth month of the campaign the Dutch and Austrians were still without their artillery. Wade boldly proposed to force Saxe's lines on the Lys: the Austrians refused. He proposed to pounce on a detachment of fourteen thousand men which Saxe had imprudently isolated from his main army: D'Arenberg carefully sent a weak body of cavalry to reveal to the detachment the danger of its position.

Finally, in the first week of October, the Allies retired into winter quarters, which was precisely the object for which D'Arenberg had been working from the first. Despite the English subsidies, he had no money with which to pay his troops, and he wished to spare the Austrian Netherlands the burden of furnishing forage and contributions. Wade, sick in body and distressed in mind, at once resigned his command. He had had enough of the Austrian alliance, and King George before long was to have enough of it also.

Once again, despite the endless length to which the war was dragging on, the establishment of the British forces remained virtually unaugmented for the year 1745. The troops allotted for service in Flanders were indeed raised to a strength of twenty-five thousand men, but this was effected only by reducing the garrison of Great Britain to fifteen thousand, which, as events were to prove before the year's end, created a situation of perilous weakness. Moreover, the past campaign had revealed a failing in one of the confederate powers which was hardly less serious than the impecuniosity and selfishness of Austria. The Dutch Army, which under Marlborough had done such brilliant service, was become hopelessly inefficient.

The competition of rival demagogues for popular favour had reduced it to such weakness in numbers that it hardly sufficed to find efficient garrisons for the fortified towns. Concurrently its discipline had suffered, and General Ligonier had already complained that the Dutch troops which served with the Allies in 1744 were intolerably insubordinate and disorderly, setting a bad example to the whole army. In February 1745 Ligonier again brought the matter to the notice of

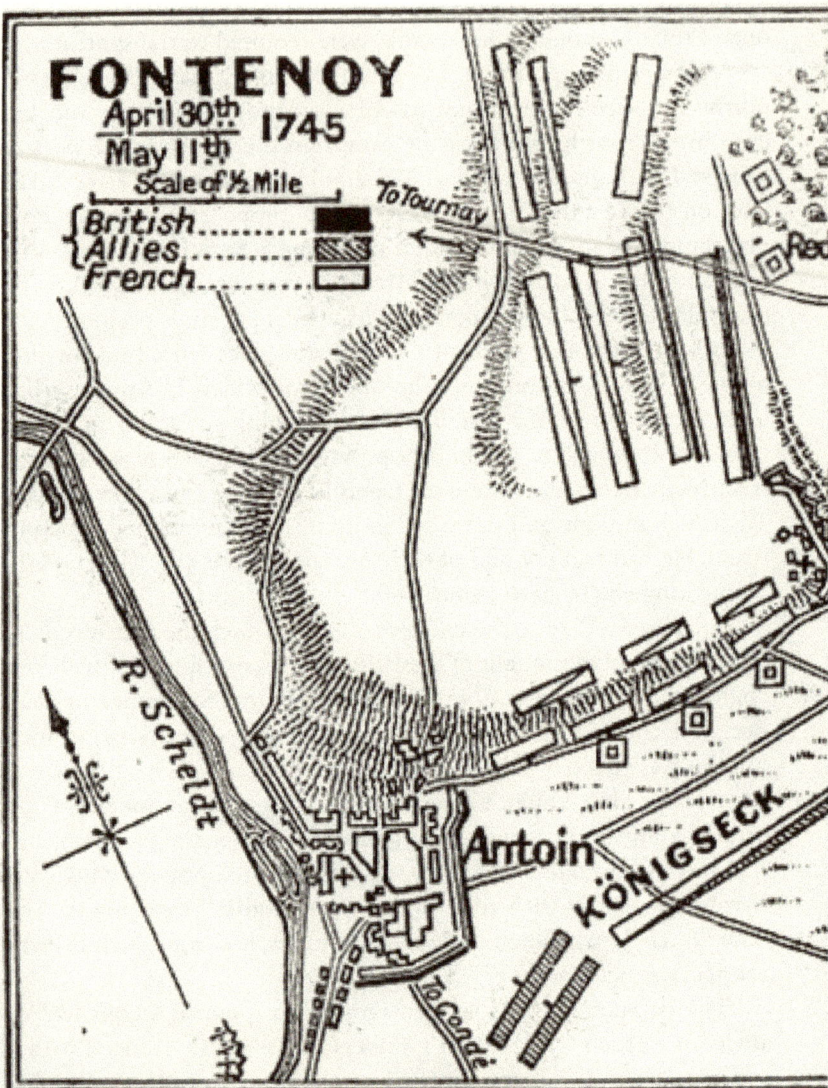

FONTENOY

April 30th 1745
May 11th

Scale of ½ Mile

British .... ▮
Allies .... ▨
French .... ▯

To Tournay

Red

R. Scheldt

Antoin

KÖNIGSECK

To Condé

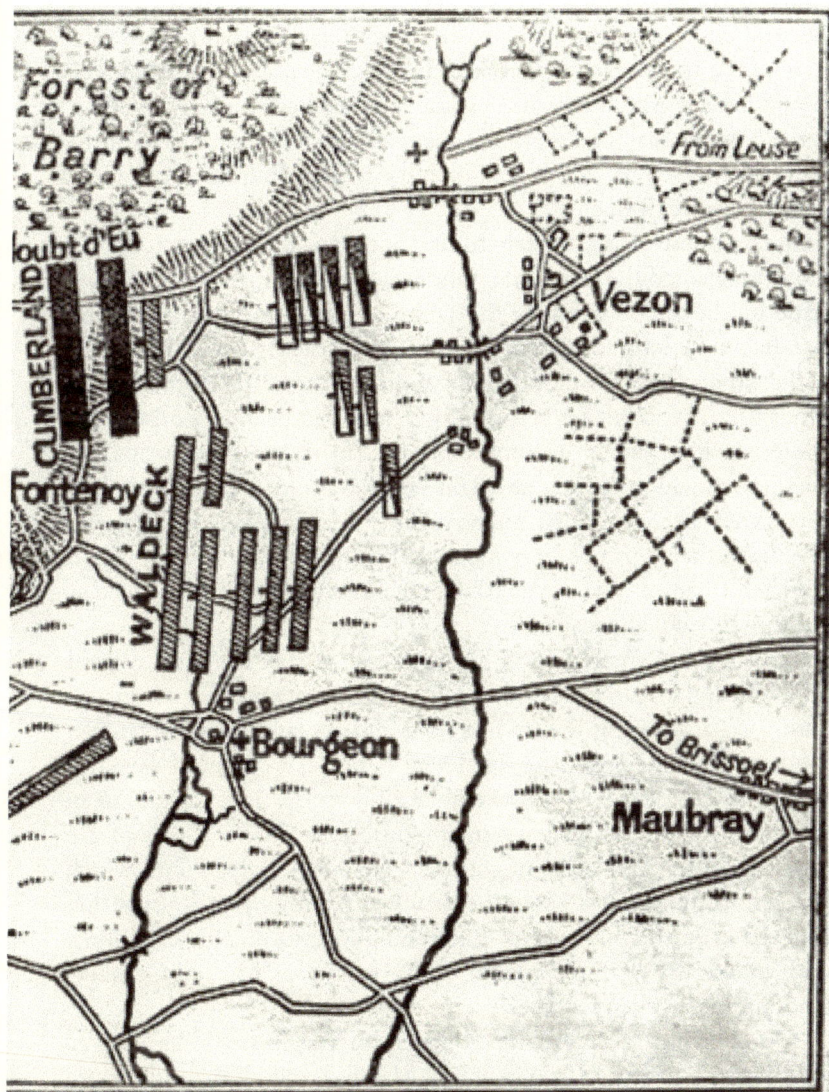

Forest of
Barry

Doubt'd'Eu

CUMBERLAND

Fontenoy

WALDECK

Bourgeon

From Leuse

Vezon

To Brissoel

Maubray

the English Government. The Dutch, he said, would probably keep all their men in garrison, and if the Allies were so weak that they could only find garrisons for the fortresses on the frontier, the French would be free to go where they pleased. It would be far better, therefore, to make a great effort, collect a hundred thousand men, take the offensive, and end the war in a single campaign. Ten thousand men would be required to guard the line of the Bruges Canal, and the remainder should besiege Maubeuge and Landreçy and enter France by the line of the Sambre, making the Meuse the main line of communication, as open alike to the passage of reinforcements from England, from Holland, and from Germany.

Such counsel was not likely to find acceptance with the men who had mismanaged the war so far. One important change, however, was made by the appointment of the Duke of Cumberland to be Commander-in-Chief in Flanders, and also in Great Britain. [1] The duke at the time of this promotion still wanted a month to complete his twenty-fifth year, but he had from his boyhood been an enthusiastic soldier, he had studied his profession, he had shown bravery at Dettingen, and, young though he might be, he was older than Condé had been when he first gained military fame. Finally, it was an immense advantage that a prince of a reigning family should preside over so motley an army as that of the Allies, since there would be the less disposition to cavil at his authority.

Cumberland entered upon his work energetically enough, crossed over to Flanders early in April, made all his arrangements for concentration at Brussels on the 2nd of May, and actually began his march southward on the following day. Even so, however, Marshal Saxe had taken the field before him, assembling his troops in Hainault, as in the previous year, so that it was impossible to divine which of the fortresses of the barrier he might intend to attack. After a feint which pointed to the siege of Mons, he marched rapidly upon Tournay and invested it on the 30th of April, screening his movements so skilfully with his cavalry that not a word of his operations reached Cumberland until nearly a week later.

Cumberland, after leaving Soignies on the 3rd of May, moved slowly south-westward by Cambron, Maulbay, and Leuse, and arrived on the evening of the 9th at Brissoel, within sight of Saxe's army. The ground immediately in front of the Allies was broken by little copses, woods, and enclosures, all of them crammed with mercenary irregular

---

1. *Gazette*, 1745.

BATTLE OF FONTENOY

troops—Pandours, Grassins, and the like—which, imitated first from the Austrians, had by this time become a necessary part of the French as of every army. Beyond this broken ground a wide plain swept in a gentle, almost unbroken slope to the village of Fontenoy, which formed the centre of Saxe's position. The advanced parties of irregulars, together with twelve squadrons drawn up on the slope before Fontenoy, forbade Cumberland's further advance for that day, and the Allies encamped for the night. Headquarters were fixed at Maubray, a village in full sight of Fontenoy, and a bare mile and a half to the south-eastward of the French camp.

On the next day the French advanced posts were pushed out of the copses, and Cumberland, together with the Prince of Waldeck and the Count of Königseck, who commanded the Dutch and the Austrians respectively, went forward to reconnoitre the position. Saxe's army occupied the crest of the slope, lying astride of the two roads that lead from Condé and from Leuse to Tournay. His right rested on the village of Anthoin and on the Scheldt, the tower of Anthoin Castle marking the western boundary of his position with clearness enough. From thence his line extended due east along the crest of the height for nearly two miles to the village of Fontenoy. A few hundred yards before Fontenoy stands the hamlet of Bourgeon, but this was now veiled in smoke and flame, having been fired by the Pandours as they retired.

From Anthoin to Fontenoy Saxe's front faced due south, but eastward from Fontenoy it turned back almost at right angles to the forest of Barry and the village of Ramecroix, fronting considerably to eastward of south. The village of Vezon, however, which lies in the same straight line with Fontenoy due east of Anthoin, was also occupied by the French as an advanced post. This was quickly cleared by Cumberland's troops, and the Allied generals completed their reconnaissance. The position was undoubtedly strong by nature and had been strengthened still further by art. Beyond Anthoin the French right flank was secured by a battery erected on the western bank of the Scheldt, while the village itself was entrenched, and held by two brigades. Between Anthoin and Fontenoy three redoubts had been constructed, and the space was defended by three brigades of infantry backed by eight squadrons of horse.

Fontenoy itself had been fortified with works and cannon, and made as strong as possible; and from Fontenoy to the forest of Barry ran a double line of entrenchments, the first line held by nine and the second by eleven battalions of infantry. At the edge of the forest of Barry were two more redoubts, the foremost of them called the Redoubt d'Eu, both armed with cannon to sweep the open space between the forest and Fontenoy; in rear of the forest were posted nine more battalions, and in rear of all two strong lines of cavalry. The flower of the French Army, both horse and foot, was stationed in this space on Saxe's left, for the English had the right of the line in the Allied Army, and Saxe knew the reputation of the red-coats.

The Allied generals decided to attack on the following day. Königseck, it is said, was for harassing Saxe's communications and compelling him to raise the siege of Tournay; but finding himself overruled by Cumberland and by Waldeck he gave way. Cumberland's force was decidedly inferior in numbers, being less than fifty thousand against fifty-six thousand men, but he was young and impetuous, and had been strongly impressed by the disastrous inaction of the preceding campaign. It was agreed that the Dutch and Austrians should assail the French centre and right, the Dutch in particular being responsible for Fontenoy, while the British attacked the French left between that village and the forest of Barry.

At two o'clock on the following morning the British began to move out of their camp upon Vezon, the cavalry leading. The advance took much time, for there were many narrow lanes to be traversed before the force could debouch upon the slope, and when the slope was passed it was still necessary to defile through the village of Vezon. Cumberland's order of attack was simple. Brigadier Ingoldsby, with the Twelfth and Thirteenth Foot, the Forty-Second Highlanders, a Hanoverian battalion, and three six-pounder cannon, was to assault the Redoubt d'Eu on the right flank of the line of the British advance, and to carry it with the bayonet. The remainder of the infantry was simply to march up across the thousand yards of open ground between it and Fontenoy and sweep the enemy out of their entrenchments.

Before five o'clock the advanced squadrons of the British horse, fifteen in all, under General Campbell, had passed through Vezon and deployed in the plain beyond, to cover the formation of the infantry for the attack. The French batteries in Fontenoy and the redoubt at once opened fire on them, but the cavalry endured the fire for an hour unmoved, until at length a shot carried away General Campbell's leg. The gallant veteran, who had fought at Malplaquet, and was now seventy-eight years of age, was carried dying from the field, full of lamentation that he could take no further part in the action. No one but himself seems to have known for what purpose his squadrons had been brought forward, and accordingly after his fall they were withdrawn.

The infantry then moved up to the front, where General Ligonier proceeded to form them in two lines, without further interruption, to use his own simple words, than a lively and murderous cannonade from the French. Cumberland meanwhile ordered up seven six-pounders to the right of the British front, which quickly came into action. Conspicuous before the French front rode an officer on a white horse, and the English gunners at once began to lay wagers who should kill him. The second or third shot brought the white charger to the ground, and his rider was carried, shattered and dying, to the rear.

He was Count Grammont, the gallant but thoughtless officer who had spoiled the combinations of Noailles at Dettingen. Then, turning to their more legitimate work, the gunners quickly made their presence felt among the French field-batteries; but the round shot never ceased to plough into the scarlet ranks of the British from Fontenoy and from the Redoubt d'Eu. Ligonier's two lines of infantry were soon formed, with the cavalry in two more lines in their rear, and the General presently sent word to Cumberland that he was ready to advance as soon as Waldeck should lead his Dutch against Fontenoy. The name of the *aide-de-camp* who carried this message should not be omitted, for he was Captain Jeffery Amherst of the First Guards.

Thereupon the Dutch and Austrians, in the centre and left, advanced against Fontenoy and Anthoin, but flinching from the fire in front, and above all from that in their flank from the battery on the other side of the Scheldt, soon shrank back under cover and could not be induced to move forward again.[2] Worst of all, the Dutch cavalry was smitten with panic, galloped back on to the top of some of the British squadrons, and fled away wildly to Hal crying out that all was lost. Things therefore went ill on the Allied left; and meanwhile on the right there was enacted a blunder still more fatal. For Ingoldsby, misconceiving his instructions, hesitated to make his attack on the Redoubt d'Eu, and despite repeated orders from Cumberland never delivered it at all. Cumberland, however, was impatient.

Without further delay he placed himself at the head of the British,

---

2. The ground immediately before Fontenoy presents for fully eight hundred yards a gentle and unbroken slope. An officer who went over the ground with me assured me that Mars la Tour itself does not offer a more perfect natural glacis for modern rifle-fire.

who were standing as Ligonier had arrayed them, in most beautiful order. In the first line, counting from right to left, stood a battalion of the First Guards, another of the Coldstreams, and another of the Scots Guards, the First, Twenty-First, Thirty-First, Eighth, Twenty-Fifth, Thirty-Third, and Nineteenth; in the second line the Buffs occupied the post of honour on the right, and next to them came in succession the Twenty-Third, Thirty-Second, Eleventh, Twenty-Eighth, Thirty-Fourth, and Twentieth. Certain Hanoverian battalions joined them on the extreme left. The drums beat, the men shouldered arms, and the detachments harnessed themselves to the two light field-guns that accompanied each battalion. Ingoldsby saw what was going forward and aligned his battalions with them on the right. Then the word was given to advance, and the two lines moved off with the slow and measured step for which they were famous in Europe.

Forward tramped the ranks of scarlet, silent and stately as if on parade. Full half a mile of ground was to be traversed before they could close with the invisible enemy that awaited them in the entrenchments over the crest of the slope, and the way was marked clearly by the red flashes and puffs of white smoke that leaped from Fontenoy and the Redoubt d'Eu on either flank. The shot plunged fiercely and more fiercely into the serried lines as they advanced into that murderous cross-fire, but the gaping ranks were quietly closed, the perfect order was never lost, the stately step was never hurried. Only the Hanoverians in the second line, finding that they were cramped for space, dropped back quietly and decorously, and marched on in third line behind the British.

Silent and inexorable the scarlet lines strode on. They came abreast of village and redoubt, and the shot which had hitherto swept away files now swept away ranks. Then the first line passed beyond redoubt and village, and the French cannon took it in reverse. The gaps grew wider and more frequent, the front grew narrower as the men closed up, but still the proud battalions advanced, strewing the sward behind them with scarlet, like some mass of red blossoms that floats down a lazy stream and sheds its petals as it goes.

At last the crest of the ridge was gained and the ranks of the French battalions came suddenly into view little more than a hundred yards distant, their coats alone visible behind the breastwork. Next to the forest of Barry, and exposed to the extreme right of the British, a line of red showed the presence of the Swiss Guards; next to them stood a line of blue, the four battalions of the French Guards, and next to the Guards a line of white, the regiments of Courtin, Aubeterre, and of the king, the choicest battalions of the French Army. Closer and closer came the British, still with arms shouldered, always silent, always with the same slow, measured tread, till they had advanced to within fifty yards of the French. Then at length Lord Charles Hay of the First Guards stepped forward with flask in hand, and doffing his hat drank politely to his enemies, he shouted:

"I hope, gentlemen, that you are going to wait for us today and not swim the Scheldt as you swam the Main at Dettingen. Men of the king's company." He continued, turning round to his own people, "these are the French Guards, and I hope you are going to beat them today"; and the English Guards answered with a cheer. The French officers hurried to the front, for the appearance of the British was a surprise to them, and called for a cheer in reply, but only a half-hearted murmur came from the French ranks, which quickly died away and gave place to a few sharp words of command; for the British were now within thirty yards.

"For what we are about to receive may the Lord make us truly thankful," murmured an English Guardsman as he looked down the barrels of the French muskets, but before his comrades round him had done laughing the French Guards had fired; and the turn of the British had come at last. [3]

For despite that deadly march through the crossfire of the French batteries to the muzzles of the French muskets, the scarlet ranks still glared unbroken through the smoke; and now the British muskets, so long shouldered, were levelled, and with crash upon crash the volleys rang out from end to end of the line, first the First Guards, then the Scots, then the Coldstreams, and so through brigade after brigade, two battalions loading while the third fired, a ceaseless, rolling, infernal fire. Down dropped the whole of the French front rank, blue coats, red coats and white, before the storm. Nineteen officers and six hundred men of the French and Swiss Guards fell at the first discharge; regiment Courtin was crushed out of existence; regiment Aubeterre, striving hard to stem the tide, was swept aside by a single imperious volley which laid half of its men on the ground.

The British infantry were perfectly in hand; their officers could be

3. Everyone knows the legend of "*Messieurs les Gardes Françaises, tirez les premiers.*" "*Non, messieurs, nous ne tirons jamais les premiers.*" But every English account agrees that the French fired first, long before the question had been raised, and I take the authority of Ligonier (who drew up the official account) as final. He says distinctly, "We received their fire."

seen coolly tapping the muskets of the men with their canes so that every discharge might be low and deadly, and nothing could withstand their fire; while the battalion-guns also poured in round after round of grape with terrible effect. The first French line was utterly shattered and broken. Even while the British were advancing Saxe had brought up additional troops to meet them and had posted regiments Couronne and Soissonois in rear of the king's regiment, and the Brigade Royal in rear of the French Guards; but all alike went down before the irresistible volleys. The red-coats continued their triumphant advance for full three hundred yards into the heart of the French camp, and old Ligonier's heart leaped within him, for he thought that the battle was won.

Saxe for his part thought little differently from Ligonier; but though half dead with dropsy, reduced to suck a bullet to assuage his intolerable thirst, so weak that he could not ride but was carried about the field in a wicker litter, the gallant German never for a moment lost his head. Sending a message to the French king, who with the *dauphin* was watching the action from a windmill in the rear, to retire across the Scheldt without delay, he strove to gain time to rally his infantry. On the first repulse of the French Guards Cumberland had detached two battalions to help the Dutch by a flanking attack on Fontenoy. Seeing that this movement must be checked at all hazards, Saxe headed these troops back by a charge of cavalry; whereupon one of the battalions extended itself along the left flank of the British. Partly in this way, partly owing to the incessant play of the French artillery on both flanks, the two British lines assumed the form of two huge oblong columns which gradually became welded into one.

The change was not untimely, for now the first line of the French cavalry, which had been posted in rear of the forest of Barry, came down upon the British at full gallop, but only to reel back shivered to fragments by the same terrible fire. Then the second line tried its fortune, but met with no better fate. Finally, the Household Cavalry, the famous *Maison du Roi*, burning with all the ardour of Dettingen unavenged, was launched against the scarlet columns, and like its predecessors, came flying back, a mob of riderless horses and uncontrollable men, decimated, shattered and repulsed by the never-ending fire.

It was like charging two flaming fortresses rather than two columns of infantry. [4]

4. *Campagnes des Pays Bas.*

Nevertheless some time was hereby gained for the broken French infantry to reform. The British, once arrived within the French camp, came to a halt, and looked at last to see how the Dutch were faring on their left. As has already been told, Waldeck's attack had been a total failure, and the British, unsupported and always under a cross-fire of artillery, fell back to the crest of the ridge and were reformed for a second attack. Waldeck undertook to make another attempt on Fontenoy, and Cumberland in reliance upon his help again advanced at the head of the British. But meanwhile Saxe had brought forward his reserves from Ramecroix, and among them the Irish brigade, to meet him, while artillery had also been brought up from the French right to play upon the British front.

The French Guards and the rest of the troops of the French first line had also been rallied, and the task of the British was well-nigh desperate. The Irish brigade, which consisted of six battalions, was made up not of Irish only but of Scots and English also, desperate characters who went into action with a rope round their necks, and would fight like devils. Yet, even in this second attack the British carried their advance as far as in the first, the perfection of their fire-discipline enabling them to beat back even the Irish brigade for a time. But their losses had been frightfully heavy; the Dutch would not move one foot to the attack of Fontenoy, and the cannonade in front added to that in the flanks became unendurable. The French infantry likewise closed round on them in superior numbers on both flanks, and it became apparent that there was nothing for it but a retreat.

Ligonier sent back two battalions to secure the roads leading through Vezon, and the retreat then began in perfectly good order. The French Household Cavalry made a furious charge upon the rear of the column as it faced about, but found to its cost that the infernal fire was not yet quenched. The three battalions of Guards and a battalion of Hanoverians turned sternly about to meet them, and gave them a few parting volleys, which wholly extinguished one regiment and brought down every officer of another. A few British squadrons, the Blues conspicuous among them, pushed forward, in spite of heavy losses, through the cross-fire to lend what help they could, and the remnant of the heroic battalions retired, facing about in succession at every hundred yards, as steadily and proudly as they had advanced.

Their losses in the action were terribly severe. Of the fifteen thousand infantry, English and Hanoverian, for the Hanoverians bore themselves not less nobly than their Allies, nearly six thousand were killed or wounded, the casualties of the twenty English battalions just exceeding four thousand men. The heaviest sufferers were the Twelfth and Twenty-Third regiments, both of which lost over three hundred men, the Twenty-First and Thirty-First, which lost rather less than three hundred men apiece, and the three battalions of Guards, which lost each of them about two hundred and fifty. Of the generals of Foot, Cumberland, Ligonier, and Brigadier Skelton, though in the hottest of the fire, alone came off unhurt; all of the rest were either killed or wounded. Many regiments of cavalry also suffered not a little, in particular the Blues and Royal Dragoons; and the total loss of the British cavalry exceeded three hundred men and six hundred horses. The loss of the French was never made public, but was certainly at least equal to that of the Allies. Contemporary accounts set it down, with no great improbability, at fully ten thousand men.

As an example of the prowess of British infantry, Fontenoy stands almost without a parallel in its history. The battalions formed under a cross-fire of artillery, remained halted under the same fire, advanced slowly for half a mile in perfect order under the same fire, and marched up to within pistol-shot of the French infantry to receive their volley before they discharged a shot. They shattered the French battalions to pieces, repulsed three separate attacks of cavalry, halted under a heavy cannonade, retired for some distance and reformed under a cross-fire, advanced again with both artillery and musketry playing on front and flanks, made the bravest brigade in the French service recoil, repelled another desperate attack of cavalry, and retired slowly and orderly under a crossfire almost to the end.

By consent of all the British commanders it was Ingoldsby's misunderstanding of his orders and his failure to capture the Redoubt d'Eu that lost the battle; and Ingoldsby was duly tried by court-martial for his behaviour. He was, however, acquitted of all but an error in judgment; and indeed there was no question of cowardice, for he accompanied the remainder of the infantry in its advance with his own detachment and was severely wounded.

It is customary to blame Cumberland for dashing his head against a wall in attempting such an attack, but he could hardly have been expected to count on such bad luck as the failure of Ingoldsby on one flank and of the Dutch on the other. The sheer audacity of his advance went near to give him the victory. Saxe owned that he never dreamed that any General would attempt such a stroke, or that any troops would execute it. Cumberland is blamed also for not attacking either the Redoubt d'Eu or Fontenoy after he had penetrated into the French camp. This charge is less easy to rebut, for the French always know when they are beaten, and seeing their left rolled up and troops advancing on Fontenoy in flank and rear would probably have given up the game for lost, and that the more readily since their ammunition in Fontenoy was for the moment nearly exhausted.

Even so, however, Saxe's reserves were always at hand at Rame-croix, and would have required to be held in check. Another puzzling question, namely, why Cumberland did not make greater use of his artillery in the action, is answered by the fact that the contractors for the horsing of the guns ran off with the horses early in the day. Such an occurrence was by no means unusual, and yet it never happened to Marlborough, not even at Malplaquet. Altogether, the conclusion seems to be that Cumberland stumbled on to a brilliant feat of arms by mistake, and, though seconded by his troops with bravery equal to his own, was not a general of sufficient capacity to turn his success to account.

At the close of the action Cumberland retreated to Ath and en-camped under the guns of that fortress, leaving his wounded to the mercy of the French, who, by a strange perversion of their usual chivalry, treated them with shameful barbarity. Among the wounded, strangely enough, were a few of the new sect of Methodists founded by John Wesley, who faced death and wounds with the stern exulta-tion that had once inspired the troopers of Cromwell. One of them wrote to Wesley, that even after a bullet in each arm had forced him to retire from the field, he hardly knew whether he was on earth or heaven, such was the sweetness of the day. This man and a few more of his kind probably helped their fellow-sufferers through the misery of the days following the battle, until Cumberland's furious remon-strances with Saxe procured for them better treatment.

From Ath Cumberland fell back to Lessines and drew out such British corps as were in garrison in Flanders to replace those which had suffered most heavily in the action. Meanwhile Tournay, very shortly after the battle, fell by treachery into the hands of the French; and Saxe's field-army being thus raised to a force nearly double that of the Allies, Cumberland was reduced to utter helplessness. The mischief of Fontenoy lay not in the repulse and the loss of men, for the British did not consider themselves to have been beaten, but in the destruc-tion of all confidence in the Dutch troops. The troubles which had harassed Wade to despair now reappeared.

Cumberland, despite his inferiority in strength, was expected somehow to defend Flanders, Brabant, and above all Brussels, and yet simultaneously to keep an active army in the field. Worse than this, he attempted to fulfil the expectation. Against his better judgment he weakened his force still further by detaching a force for the garrison of Mons, and then, instead of taking up a strong position on the Scheldt to cover Ghent at all hazards, he yielded to the pressure of the Austrians and crossed the Dender to cover Brussels.

Halting too long between two opinions he at last sent off a detachment for the defence of Ghent, half of which was cut off and turned back with heavy loss, while the other half, after enduring much rough usage on the march, entered Ghent only to see the town surprised by the French on the following day. Four British regiments took part in this unlucky enterprise and suffered heavy loss, while the Royal Scots and the Twenty-Third, which had been despatched to Ghent after Fontenoy, of course became prisoners. Moreover, a vast quantity of British military stores were captured in Ghent, although Cumberland had a week before ordered that they should be removed. After this blow Cumberland retired to Vilvorde, a little to the north of Brussels, still hoping to cover both that city and Antwerp, and so to preserve his communications both with Germany and with the sea.

Here again he sacrificed his better judgment to the clamour of the Austrians, for he would much have preferred to secure Antwerp only. His position was in fact most critical, and he was keenly alive to it. Just when his anxiety was greatest there came a letter from the Secretary of State, announcing that invasion of England was imminent, and hoping that troops could be spared from Flanders without prejudice to his operations. Ligonier answered indignantly:

> What! Are you aware that the enemy has seventy thousand men against our thirty thousand, and that they can place a superior force on the canal before us and send another army round between us and Antwerp to cut off our supplies and force us to fight at a disadvantage? This is our position, and this is the result of providing His Royal Highness with insufficient troops; and yet you speak of our having a corps to spare to defend England!

Saxe's plan for reducing the Allies was in fact uniformly the same throughout the whole of the war, namely to cut off their communications with the sea on one side and with Germany on the other. Even before he began to press Cumberland northward toward Antwerp he had detached a force to lay siege to Ostend, which was the English base. Cumberland, on his side, had advised that the dykes should be broken down and the country inundated in order to preserve it, and both Dutch and Austrians had promised that this should be done; but as usual it was not done, and before the end of August Ostend had surrendered to the French. The English base was then perforce shifted to Antwerp. But by this time, (August), the requests for the return of troops to England had become urgent and imperative orders. First ten battalions were recalled, then the rest of the foot, (Sept.-Oct), and at last practically the whole of the army, including Cumberland himself. It is now time to explain the causes for the alarm in England.

CHAPTER 4

Roucoux & Lauffeld

The virtual evacuation of the Low Countries by the British in consequence of the Jacobite Rebellion, in 1745, was an advantage too obvious to be overlooked by the French. At the end of January, 1746, though winter-quarters were not yet broken up, they severed the communication between Antwerp and Brussels, and a week later took the town of Brussels itself by escalade. The citadel, after defending itself for a fortnight, went the way of the town, and the capital of the Spanish Netherlands was turned into a French place of arms. The consternation in Holland was great, and it was increased when the French presently besieged and captured Antwerp.

Meanwhile the British commander, Lord Dunmore, who had been left in the Netherlands with a few squadrons of cavalry, could only look on in utter helplessness. It was not until June that the Hessian troops in British pay and a few British battalions could be embarked, together with General Ligonier to command them, from England; and it was not until July, owing to foul winds, that they were finally landed at Williamstadt. The change of base was significant in itself, for since the capture of Ostend and Antwerp there was no haven for British ships except in the United Provinces.

Even after the disembarkation these forces were found to be still unready to take the field. The Hessians had not a grain of powder among them, and there were neither horses for the artillery nor waggons for the baggage. Again, to add small difficulties to great, the Austrian General, Batthyany, having no British officer as his peer in command, denied to the British troops the place of honour at the right of the line. It was a trifling matter, but yet sufficient to embarrass counsel, destroy harmony, and delay operations.

While the Allies were thus painfully drawing their forces together, the activity of the French never ceased. The Prince of Conti was detached with a considerable force to the Haine, where he quickly reduced Mons and St. Ghislain, thus throwing down almost the last relics of the Austrian barrier in the south. Thence moving to the Sambre, Conti laid siege to Charleroi. It was now sufficiently clear that the plan of the French campaign was to operate on the line of the Meuse for the invasion of Holland. Maestricht once taken, the rest would be easy, for most of the Dutch army were prisoners in the hands of the French; and with the possession of the line of the Meuse communication between the Allied forces of England and of Austria would be cut off. But before Maestricht could be touched Namur must first be captured; and the campaign of 1746 accordingly centred about Namur.

For the first fortnight of July the Allies remained at Terheyden, a little to the north of Breda, Saxe's army lying some thirty miles southwestward of them about Antwerp. On the 17th of July the Allies at last got on march, still with some faint hopes of saving Charleroi, and proceeded south-eastward, a movement which Saxe at once parried by marching parallel with them to the Dyle between Arschot and Louvain. Pushing forward, despite endless difficulties of transport and forage, through a wretched barren country, the Allies, now under command of Prince Charles of Lorraine, reached Peer, turned southward across the Demer at Hasselt, and by the 27th of July were at Borchloen. They were thus actually on the eastern side of the French main army, within reach of the Mehaigne and not without good hope of saving Namur if not Charleroi.

On the 1st of August they crossed the Mehaigne, only to learn to their bitter disappointment that Charleroi had surrendered that very morning. Saxe meanwhile, with the principal part of his army, still lay entrenched at Louvain with detachments pushed forward to Tirlemont and Gembloux. The Allies continued their march before the eyes of these detachments to Masy on the Orneau, and there took up a position between that river and the head-waters of the Mehaigne, fronting to the north-east. This was the line approved through many generations of war as the best for the protection of Namur.

Saxe now drew nearer to them, and the two armies lay opposite to each other, in many places not more than a musket-shot apart, both entrenched to the teeth. The Allies so far had decidedly scored a success, but they were outnumbered by the French by three to two, and they were confined within a narrow space wherein subsistence was extremely difficult; while if they moved, Namur was lost. Ligonier, who was most uneasy over the situation, longed for five thousand cavalry with which to make a dash at Malines and so call the enemy back in haste to defend Brussels and Antwerp. Prince Charles, however, was averse to operations of such a nature. His hope was that Saxe would offer him battle on the historic plain of Ramillies where, notwithstanding the disparity of numbers, he trusted that the quality of his troops and the traditions of the field would enable him to prevail. But Saxe had no intention of doing anything of the kind. He did indeed shift his position further to the north and east, with the field of Ramillies in his rear, but it was not to offer battle.

Pushing out detachments to eastward he captured Huy, and cutting off the Allies' communications with Liége and Maestricht forced them to cross the Meuse and fall back on Maestricht from the other side of the river. Cross the Meuse the Allies accordingly did, unmolested, to Ligonier's great relief, by twenty thousand French who were stationed on the eastern bank of the stream. They then opened communication with Maestricht, five leagues away, while Saxe extended his army comfortably with its face to the eastward along the line of the Jaar from Warem to Tongres, waiting till want of forage should compel the Allies to recross the Meuse. Back they came over the river within a fortnight, as he had expected, and the Marshal, without attempting to dispute the passage, retreated quietly for a few miles, knowing full well that his enemy could not follow him from lack of bread. Ligonier never in his life longed so intensely for the end of a campaign.

On the 17th of September the Allies advanced upon the French and offered battle. Saxe answered by retiring to an impregnable position between Tongres and the Demer. There was no occasion for him to fight, when his enemies were short of provisions and their cavalry was going to ruin from want of forage. So there the two armies remained once more, within sight of each other but unwilling to fight, since an attack on the entrenchments of either host would have entailed the certain destruction of the attacking force. But meanwhile the trenches had been opened before Namur by a French corps under the Prince of Clermont, and within nine days the town had fallen. Ligonier again urged his design, for which he had prepared the necessary magazines, to upset Saxe's plans by a dash upon Antwerp, but he could find no support in the council of war; so there was nothing for the Allies to do but to wait until some further French success should compel them to move.

Such a success was not long in coming. The castle of Namur surrendered after a miserable defence of but eleven days; Clermont's corps was released for operations in the field, and the Allies were forced to fall back for the protection of Liége. Accordingly, on the 7th of October they crossed the Jaar, not without annoyance from the enemy, and took up a new position, which gave them indeed possession of Liége, but placed them between the Meuse in their rear, and an enemy of nearly twice their strength on the Jaar before their front.

Now at last Saxe resolved to strike a blow. On the 10th of October he crossed the Jaar with evident intention of an attack, and the Allied army received orders to be ready for action before the following dawn. The Allies' position faced very nearly due west, the army being drawn up astride of the two paved roads leading into Liége from Tongres and St. Trond. Their extreme right rested on the Jaar and was covered by the villages of Slins, Fexhe, and Enick, all of which were strongly entrenched and occupied by the Austrians.

South of Enick extended an open plain from that village to the village of Liers, and in this plain was posted the Hanoverian infantry and four British battalions, the Eighth, Nineteenth, Thirty-Third, and Forty-Third Foot, with the Hessian infantry on their left in rear of Liers. The Hanoverian cavalry prolonged the line southward to the village of Varoux, and the Sixth and Seventh Dragoons and Scots Greys continued it to the village of Roucoux, from which point Dutch troops carried it on to the village of Ance, which formed the extreme left of the position. Ligonier did not like the situation, for he did not see how the turning of the left flank could be prevented if, as would certainly be the case, the French should seriously attempt it.

Prince Charles, knowing that if his right were turned his retreat to Maestricht would be cut off, had taken care to hold the right flank in real strength and dared not weaken it; but the position, with the Meuse in its rear, was perilously shallow, while the convergence of two ravines from the Jaar and Melaigne into its centre allowed of but one narrow way of communication between the right and left of the army. The defects of the Allies' dispositions were in fact not unlike those which had proved fatal to King William at Landen, and Ligonier's anxiety was proved to rest on all too good foundation.

The morning of the 11th of October opened with bad news for the Allies. The French had been admitted into Liége by the inhabitants behind the backs of the Dutch, so that the Prince of Waldeck, who commanded on the left, was obliged to withdraw eight battalions from Roucoux and post them *en potence* on his left flank, with his cavalry

in support. Thus the defence of Roucoux, as well as of Liers and Varoux, was left to eight battalions of British, Hanoverians, and Hessians
only. This made the outlook for the Allied left the worse, since it was
evident that the brunt of the French attack would fall upon it. Saxe
gave Prince Charles little time for reflection. He had one hundred
and twenty thousand men against eighty thousand, and he knew that
of the eighty thousand at least one-third were tied to the Austrian
entrenchments about the Jaar. He opened the action by a furious assault upon the Dutch on the left flank, his infantry being formed in
dense columns, so that the attack could be renewed continually by
fresh troops. Simultaneously fifty-five battalions in three similar columns were launched upon Liers, Varoux, and Roucoux. Outmatched
though they were, Dutch, Germans, and British all fought splendidly
and repelled more than one attack.

But, to use Ligonier's words, as soon as two French brigades had
been repulsed in each village, a third brigade ran in; and the eight
battalions, though they still held Liers, were forced to withdraw both
from Roucoux and Varoux. Being rallied, however, by Ligonier, they
advanced again and recaptured both villages; and the Nineteenth and
Forty-Third took up a position in a hollow road which they held to
the last. The Dutch now began to retire across the rear of the position from the left, in good order despite heavy losses, while Ligonier
checked the enemy in the plain with the British cavalry. When the
Dutch had passed he ordered his own men to retreat in the same
direction, still covering the movement with the cavalry and with the
Thirteenth and Twenty-sixth Foot, which had been sent to the field
from the garrison of Maestricht. The Austrians formed a rear-guard
in turn when the British and their German comrades had passed, and
thus the whole army filed off, unpursued and in perfect order, and
crossed the Meuse in safety on the following morning.

The action may be looked upon as a fortunate escape for the Allies,
since it was impossible, humanly speaking, that it could have issued
favourably for them. Prince Charles, in seeking to cover both Liége
and Maestricht, had attempted too much. His army thus occupied too
wide a front, the villages in the centre were too weakly held, there was
hardly anywhere a second line of infantry, and the left flank could not
be sustained against so superior an enemy. The total loss of the Allies
was about five thousand men, which was sufficiently severe considering that but a third of the army was engaged. The casualties of the
British were three hundred and fifty killed and wounded, of whom no

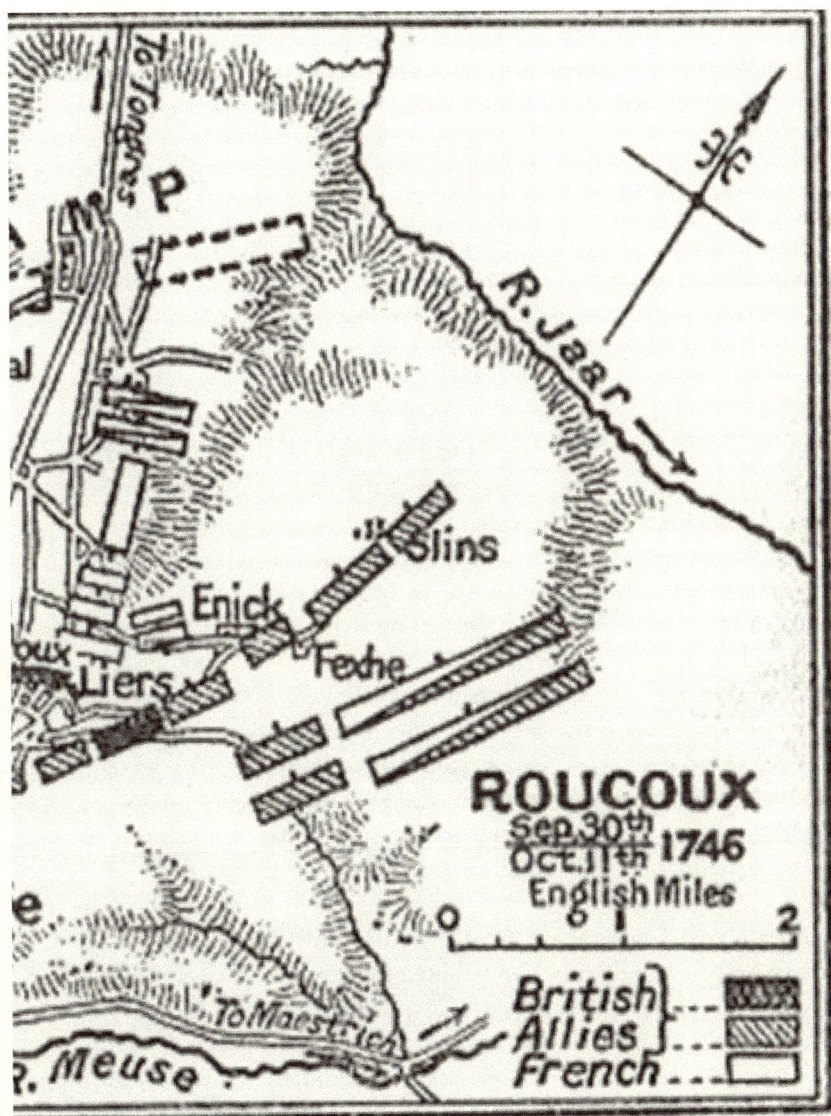

P

To Tongres

R. Jaar

·lins

Enick

Feche

·oux

Liers

ROUCOUX

Sep 30th
Oct.11th 1746

English Miles

0   1   2

To Maestrich

R. Meuse

British ....
Allies ....
French ....

fewer than two hundred belonged to the Forty-Third.

The French lost as many men as the Allies, or more, and gained little by the action except eight guns captured from the British, Hanoverians, and Hessians. Had not the Allied troops been far better in quality and discipline than the French, they must have been lost during their retreat with superior numbers both in flank and rear. Both armies presently retired into winter-quarters, and the campaign ended far less disastrously an might have been feared for the Allies.

Unfortunately, however, it was not in Flanders only that discredit fell upon the British arms. At the end of September a force of six battalions was sent, under command of General St. Clair, to the coast of Brittany to attack Port L'Orient and destroy the stores of the French East India Company there. The enterprise was conducted with amazing feebleness. The troops landed at Quimperle Bay practically unopposed, but, being fired at on their march on the following day, were turned loose to the plunder of a small town as a punishment to the inhabitants for their resistance. On the following day they reached L'Orient, which the deputy governor of the East India Company offered to surrender on good terms.

His overtures, however, were rejected and a siege was begun in form; but after a few days of firing and the loss of about a hundred men killed and wounded, St. Clair thought it prudent to retreat; and on the 12th of October the troops re-embarked and returned to England. Anything more pointless than the design or more contemptible than the execution of this project can hardly be conceived, for it simply employed regiments, which were badly needed in Flanders and America, in useless operations which did not amount to a diversion.

If the cause of Queen Maria Theresa was to be saved, it was evident that great efforts were imperative in the coming campaign of 1747. To meet the vast numbers brought into the field by the French the Austrians promised to have sixty thousand men at Maseyck on the Meuse by April; the British contributed four regiments of cavalry and fourteen battalions of infantry; and it was hoped that the Allies would take the field with a total strength of one hundred and ten battalions, one hundred and sixty squadrons, and two hundred and twenty guns, besides irregular troops, the whole to be under command of the Duke of Cumberland. Unfortunately the weather was adverse to an early opening of the campaign; and the French, by the seizure of Cadsand and Sluys, which were shamefully surrendered by the Dutch, closed the southern mouth of the Scheldt below Antwerp.

This was a sad blow to the arrangements for the transport of the Allies, since it brought about the necessity of hauling all the forage for the British overland from Breda. Had Cumberland been in a position to open the campaign before the French, he meant to have laid siege to Antwerp; as things were, he was compelled, thanks chiefly to the apathy of the Dutch, to attempt to bring Saxe to a general action. His last letter before beginning operations has, however, an interest of another kind. It contains a recommendation that Major James Wolfe may be permitted to purchase a vacant lieutenant-colonelcy in the Eighth Foot, that officer having served constantly and well during the past two years as a major of brigade and proved himself capable and desirous to do his duty.

The French being encamped between Malines and Louvain, Cumberland collected his troops at Tilburg and advanced straight upon them, encamping on the 26th of May on the Great Nethe, a little to the east of Antwerp, between Lierre and Herenthout. Saxe, entrenched as usual to the teeth, remained immovable for three weeks, and Cumberland despaired of bringing him to action. At length the news that a detached corps of thirty thousand French, under the Prince of Clermont, was on the old ground about Tongres, moved Cumberland to march to the Demer, in the hope of overwhelming Clermont before Saxe could join him. Saxe, however, was on his guard, and on the 29th of June prepared to concentrate the whole of his army at Tongres. Cumberland thereupon decided to take up Saxe's camp of the previous year, from Bilsen, on the headwaters of the Demer, to Tongres.

So sending forward Count Daun, afterwards well known as an antagonist of Frederick the Great, with a corps of Austrians to occupy Bilsen, he ordered the rest of the army to follow as quickly as possible on the next day. Riding forward at daybreak of the morrow, Cumberland was dismayed to see the French advancing in two columns from Tongres, as if to fall upon the head of his own army.[1] This was a surprise. Cumberland knew that Saxe was in motion but had not expected him so soon; and indeed Saxe had made a notable march, for his army had not left Louvain until the 29th of June and had traversed little less than fifty miles in two days.

The duke lost no time in setting such troops as were on the spot in order of battle, and hurried away to see if those on the march could be brought up in time to force back the French, and to secure the posi-

1. Cumberland blamed the Austrian General, Baroney, and his irregulars for supine negligence on the march.

tion of his choice. But the French cavalry was too quick for him, and, before Ligonier could bring up the English horse, had occupied the centre of the ground which Cumberland had intended for himself.

Ligonier drew up his squadrons before them to bar their further advance, and the Allied infantry, as it came up, was formed in order of battle, fronting, however, not to eastward, as had been originally designed, but almost due south. In fact, owing to Saxe's unexpected arrival and to deficient arrangements by the staff of the Allies, there seems to have been considerable delay in putting the Allied army into any formation at all, or the French might certainly have been forced back to Tongres. Saxe's rear had not yet come up and the men were fatigued by a long and harassing march; but Cumberland was not the man to fight an action of the type of Oudenarde, and the opportunity was lost.

The position now occupied by the Allies extended from some rising ground known as the Commanderie, a little to the south-east of Bilsen, along a chain of villages and low heights to the Jaar, a little to the south of Maestricht. The Commanderie being the right of the line was held by the Austrians, with a strong corps thrown back *en potence* to Bilsen to protect the right flank; for it was as important on this field as on that of Roucoux that the retreat into Holland should not be cut off. The ground possessed natural features of strength which were turned to good account, so good account indeed that the Allied right, like the French left at Ramillies, could neither attack nor be attacked. Eastward from the Commanderie the Austrians occupied the heights of Spaeven, together with the villages of Gross and Klein Spaeven; next to them the Dutch formed the centre of the line, while the Hanoverians and British held the villages of Val, or Vlytingen, and Lauffeld, and prolonged the line to its extreme left at the village of Kesselt.

There the Allies lay on their arms until nightfall, while Saxe's weary battalions tramped on till far into the night up to their bivouacs. At daybreak the French were seen to be in motion, marching and countermarching in a way that Cumberland did not quite understand; the fact being that Saxe, as at Roucoux, was doubling the left wing of his army in rear of the right, for the formation of those dense columns of attack which he could handle with such consummate skill. After observing them until nine o'clock Cumberland came to the conclusion that the marshal meditated no immediate movement and retired to the Commanderie for breakfast; but he had hardly sat down when an urgent message arrived from Ligonier that the enemy was on the point of attacking.

Cumberland at once returned and moved the left of his line somewhat forward, setting fire to the village of Vlytingen and occupying Lauffeld with three British and two Hessian battalions. Lauffeld was a straggling village a quarter of a mile long, covered by a multitude of small enclosures with mud walls about six feet high, topped by growing hedges. It was thus easily turned into a strong post for infantry, and cannon were posted both in its front and flanks. The remainder of the British were drawn up for the most part in rear of Lauffeld in order to feed and relieve its garrison, the brigade of Guards being posted in the hedges before Vlytingen. The British cavalry stood on the left of the infantry and joined their line to that of the Dutch.

Meanwhile Saxe, sending forward a cloud of irregular troops to mask his movements, had despatched Count d'Estrées and the Count of Segur with a strong force of infantry and cavalry to seize the villages of Montenaken and Wilre on the left flank of the Allies. This service was performed with little loss. At the same time he directed the Marquis of Salières, with six brigades of foot and twenty guns, to attack Vlytingen, and launched five brigades, with as many guns, backed by a large force of cavalry, against Lauffeld. The assault of the French infantry upon Lauffeld was met by a furious resistance. It was just such another struggle as that of Neerwinden, from hedge to hedge and from wall to wall; and the French, for all their superiority of numbers, were driven back headlong from the village with terrible loss.

Salières met with little better success against the brigade of Guards in the hedges of Vlytingen; but with great readiness he turned half of his guns to his right against Lauffeld and the remainder against a ravine on his left, with most destructive effect. Cumberland, observing the fury with which Saxe had concentrated his attack against these two villages, asked the Austrians to relieve him by a diversion upon his right; but the Austrian troops could not face the fire of Salières' guns, and it became clear that Vlytingen and Lauffeld must be held by the British and Hanoverians alone.

Saxe's first attack had been brilliantly repulsed. He at once replaced the beaten troops by two fresh brigades of infantry, with cavalry to support them, and renewed the assault, but with no better success. The British were driven back from the outer defences only to stand more fiercely by those within, and Lauffeld remained unconquered. But Saxe was not to be deterred from his purpose. Two more brigades, including the six Irish battalions that had saved the day at Fontenoy, were added to those already on the spot, and the whole of them launched

61

for a third attack against Lauffeld. They were met by the same stubborn resistance and the same deadly fire; and the Irish brigade lost no fewer than sixty officers in the struggle. Nevertheless Irish impetuosity carried the rest of the troops forward; the British were borne back to the rearmost edge of the village and the French began to swarm up the slope beyond it. Cumberland promptly ordered the whole of his line of infantry to advance; and the French at once gave way before them. The French cavalry was obliged to drive the foot forward at the sword's point, but Cumberland continued steadily to gain ground despite their efforts.

Then at an unlucky moment, some Dutch squadrons in the centre were seized with panic and came galloping straight into the British line, carried away the Hessians and one squadron of the Greys and fell pell-mell upon the Twenty-First and Twenty-Third Fusiliers. The Twenty-First, anticipating the treatment of the Belgians at Waterloo, gave the Dutchmen a volley and partly saved themselves, but the Twenty-Third suffered terribly and the whole line was thrown into confusion. Before order could be restored Salières had thrown three more brigades upon Lauffeld, which closed in round it, blocking up a hollow road which formed the entrance into it from the rear, and barring the way for all further reinforcements of the Allies. The few troops that were left in the village were speedily overpowered, and Lauffeld was lost.

Some of Daun's Austrians now advanced to Cumberland's help from the right; but three French brigades of cavalry that were waiting before Vlytingen at once moved forward to check them, and charging boldly into them succeeded in turning them back, though themselves roughly handled when retiring from the charge. Meanwhile Saxe had brought up ten guns to right and left of Lauffeld, and reinforcing the cavalry of D'Estrées and Segur extended it in one long line from Lauffeld to Wilre, for a final crushing attack on the Allied left. Order had been restored among the British infantry, who were now retreating with great steadiness, but they were wholly unsupported. Ligonier, determined to save them at any cost, caught up the Greys, Inniskillings, and Cumberland's dragoons, and led them straight against the masses of the French cavalry.

The gallant brigade charged home, crashed headlong through the horse, and fell upon the infantry beyond, but being galled by their fire and attacked in all quarters by other French squadrons, was broken past all rallying and very heavily punished. Ligonier himself was overthrown and taken prisoner. Cumberland, who had plunged into the broken ranks to try to rally them, was cut off by the French dragoons, and only with difficulty contrived to join the remainder of his cavalry on the left. With these he covered the retreat of the army, which was successfully effected in good order and with little further loss.

So ended the Battle of Lauffeld, in which the British bore the brunt with a firmness that extorted the praise even of Frenchmen, but of which few Englishmen have ever heard. The troops, in Cumberland's words, behaved one and all so well that he could not commend any one regiment without doing injustice to the rest. The total loss of the five regiments of horse and fourteen battalions of foot was close upon two thousand men. [2] The three devoted regiments which charged with Ligonier were the worst sufferers, the Greys losing one hundred and sixty men, the Inniskillings one hundred and twenty, and Cumberland's dragoons nearly one hundred. The loss of the whole of the Allies was about six thousand men, that of the French decidedly greater, amounting indeed, according to Saxe's account, to not less than ten thousand men. The British, moreover, had nine French colours and five French standards as trophies for their consolation. Finally, the French failed to accomplish the object of the action, which was to cut off the Allies from Maestricht.

After the battle the Allies crossed the Meuse and encamped at Heer, a little to the east of Maestricht, while Saxe returned to his quarters at Tongres. The French then detached a corps for the capture of Bergen op Zoom; but the most important transactions of the war still went forward on the Meuse, where constant negotiations were carried on between Saxe and Cumberland. The campaign closed with the fall of Bergen op Zoom and the capture of most of the strong places in Dutch Brabant.

By this time King George and his people in England were thoroughly sick of the war. The British had suffered severely in every action, but had reaped no success except in the fortunate victory of Dettingen. The Dutch had proved themselves useless and contemptible as Allies, their government feeble and corrupt in council, their troops unstable if not dangerous in action. The Austrians, in spite of lavish subsidies, had never furnished the troops that they had promised, and

---

2. The regiments present at Lauffeld were the Greys, 4th Hussars, Inniskillings, 7th Hussars, and Cumberland's dragoons, one battalion each of the 1st and 3rd Guards, 3rd, 4th, 13th, 19th, 21st, 23rd, 25th, 32nd, 33rd, 36th, 37th, 48th Foot. The two last had no casualties.

LAUFFELD
June 21st
July 2nd 1747
English Miles

0   1   2

British ......
Allies ......
French ......

Bilsen

R. Demer

AUSTRIANS
Klein Spaeven
The Commanderie
Gross Spaeven
DUTCH
Vlytingen

To Tongres

Maestricht

To Heer

Wyk

Kesselt

Wilre

Lauffeld

R. Jaar

Montenaken

R. Meuse

had invariably obstructed operations through the obstinacy of their generals and the selfishness of their ends. The opening of the campaign of 1748 was even more unpromising for the Allies. Saxe, strong in the possession of a superior force, kept Cumberland in suspense between apprehensions for Breda and for Maestricht, and when finally he laid siege to Maestricht could match one hundred and fifteen thousand men against Cumberland's five-and-thirty thousand. War on such terms against such a master as Saxe was ridiculous.

Moreover, the Dutch, despite a recent revolution, were more supine than ever; the Prince of Orange, who was the new ruler, actually keeping two thousand of his troops from the field that they might adorn the baptism of one of his babies. In the face of such facts Cumberland pressed earnestly for peace; and on the 30th of April preliminaries were signed, which six months later were expanded into the definite treaty of Aix-la-Chapelle.

The peace left matters practically as they had stood before the war, with the significant exception that Frederick the Great retained Silesia. Not a word was said as to the regulation of trade between England and Spain, which had been the original ground of quarrel; and as between England and France it was agreed that there should be mutual restitution of all captures. Yet this could not set the two countries in the same position as before the war. The French were utterly exhausted; but the British, though not a little harassed by the cost of maintaining armies and producing subsidies, had received a military training which was to stand them in good stead for the great struggle that lay before them. To understand this struggle aright it must first be seen what was implied by the mutual restitution of all captures, for among the possessions that had changed hands during the war were Cape Breton and Madras.

Conflict between Britain and France was by no means suspended but the theatres of operation moved across the oceans as both powers sought to establish their respective empires. America and India were the scenes of fierce struggle whilst the impending conflagration in Europe simmered for another seven years.

CHAPTER 5

The Outbreak of the Seven Years' War

By the close of the year 1755 hostilities were in full play between English and French in North America. Yet war had not been declared, nor, though it was certain to come, had any preparation been made for it. The measures taken at the beginning of 1755 sufficiently indicate the feebleness and vacillation of a foolish and effete Administration. In February some addition had been made to the infantry by raising the strength of the Guards and of seven regiments of the Line; and in March the king sent a message to Parliament requesting an augmentation of the forces by land and sea. The Ministry employed the powers thus given to them in raising five thousand marines in fifty independent companies, and placing them expressly under the command of the Lord High Admiral. It is said, (Walpole), that Newcastle refused to raise new regiments from jealousy of the Duke of Cumberland's nomination of officers, and there is nothing incredible in the assertion.

But though this measure pointed at least to activity on the part of the fleet, never were British ships employed to less purpose. The squadron sent out under Boscawen to intercept the French reinforcements on their way to Louisburg was considerably inferior to the enemy's fleet, and required to be reinforced, of course at the cost of confusion and delay, before it was fit to fulfil its duty. Fresh trouble was caused in May by the king's departure for Hanover, a pleasure which he refused to deny himself despite the critical state of affairs in England. During his absence his power was delegated, as was customary, to a Council of Regency, a body which was always disposed to reserve matters of importance for the king's decision, and was doubly infirm of purpose with such a creature as Newcastle among its ruling spirits.

67

A powerful fleet under Sir Edward Hawke was ready for sea and for action; and the Duke of Cumberland, remembering the consequences of peaceful hostility in 1742 and 1743, was for throwing off the mask, declaring open war and striking swiftly and at once. He was, however, overruled, and Hawke's fleet was sent to sea with instructions that bound it to a violation of peace and a travesty of war. The king meanwhile was solicitous above all things for the security of Hanover. Subsidiary treaties with Bavaria and Saxony for the protection of the Electorate had for some time existed, but were expired or expiring; and now that some return for the subsidies of bygone years seemed likely to be required, the contracting States stood out for better terms. The king therefore entered into a new treaty with Hesse-Cassel for the supply of eight thousand men, and with Russia for forty thousand more, in the event of the invasion of Hanover.

With these treaties in his pocket he returned to England, Sept. 15, to find the nation full of alarm and discontent. Nor was the nation at fault in its feelings. In August the news of Braddock's defeat had arrived and had been received with impotent dismay. Yet nothing was done to retrieve the disaster, and two full months passed before a few thousand men were added to all three arms of the army. Twenty battalions of the Line raised to a strength of a thousand men each; eleven regiments of cavalry augmented; two new companies added to the artillery, (*Miscellaneous Orders*, October 1755. *Warrant Books*, 21st October 1755).

Meanwhile Newcastle, after vainly endeavouring to persuade Pitt to serve under him, had strengthened his Ministry somewhat by securing the accession of Henry Fox; and on the 13th of November the king opened Parliament, announcing, as well he might, the speedy approach of war. A long debate followed, wherein Pitt surpassed himself in denunciation of subsidiary treaties and contemptuous condemnation of Newcastle; but the party of the Court was too strong for him, and the treaties were confirmed by a large majority. Pitt was dismissed from his office of Paymaster, and Fox having been promoted to be Secretary of State was succeeded by Lord Harrington as Secretary at War. Lastly, some weeks later, General Ligonier was most unjustly ousted from the post of Master-General of the Ordnance, to make way for a place-hunter who was not ashamed thus to disgrace his honoured title of Duke of Marlborough. It seemed, in fact, as though there were a general conspiracy to banish ability from high station.

A fortnight later, Nov. 27, the estimates for the army were submitted to Parliament. Notwithstanding the urgent danger of the situation, the number of men proposed on the British Establishment little exceeded thirty-four thousand men for Great Britain and thirteen thousand for the colonies. A few days afterwards, Dec. 5, the question was debated, and Barrington then announced a further increase of troops; whereupon Pitt very pertinently asked the unanswerable question why all these augmentations were made so late. The House, however, was in earnest as to the military deficiencies of the country. Fox had taunted Pitt by challenging him to bring forward a Militia Bill, Dec. 8, and Pitt seized the opportunity offered by a debate on the Militia to give the outlines of a scheme for making that force more efficient. His proposals were embodied in a Bill, which formed the basis of the Militia Act that was to be passed, as shall be seen, in the following year. So far therefore the Commons forced upon the Government and the country at least the consideration of really valuable work.

On the re-assembly of Parliament after Christmas an estimate was presented for the formation of ten new regiments, to be made up in part of certain supplementary companies which had been added to existing battalions in 1755. These new regiments were, in order of seniority, Abercromby's, Napier's, Lambton's, Whitmore's, Campbell's, Perry's, Lord Charles Manner's, Arabin's, Anstruther's and Montagu's, and they are still with us numbered in succession the Fiftieth to the Fifty-Ninth, (*Miscellaneous Orders*, 7th January 1756). At the same time a new departure was made by adding a light troop apiece to eleven regiments of dragoons, both men and horses being specially equipped for the work which is now expected of all cavalry, but which was then entrusted chiefly to irregular horse formed upon the model of the Austrian Hussars.

Yet another novelty was foreshadowed in February when a bill was introduced to enable the king to grant commissions to foreign Protestants in America. The origin of this measure, according to Horace Walpole, was a proposal made by one Prevost, a Protestant refugee, to raise four battalions of Swiss and Provincials in America, with a British officer for colonel-in-chief but with a fair number of foreigners holding other commissions. Quite as probably this new step was quickened, if not suggested, by the news that the French contemplated the enlistment of recruits among the foreign population of British America. The vote for these four battalions was passed without a division, though Pitt opposed the bill with all his power and was supported by a petition from the Agent of Massachusetts. He was vehement for the employment of British soldiers to fight British battles; whereas so far the most important military measure of king and ministers had been the hiring of Germans. The bill was none the less passed, and on the 4th of March the order for the enlistment of the four battalions was given. Lord Loudoun was to be their colonel-in-chief, Pennsylvania their recruiting-ground, and their title the Royal Americans, an appellation long since displaced by the famous number of the Sixtieth.

Amid all these preparations, however, the nation throughout the first months of 1756 lived in abject terror of an invasion. France on her side had not been backward in equipping herself for the approaching contest. Great activity at Toulon had been followed by equal activity at Dunkirk, and despite good information as to the true object of the armaments fitted out at these two ports, the people naturally, and the Government most culpably, persisted in the belief that they were designed for a descent upon Britain herself. Few troops were ready to meet such a descent, for votes cannot improvise trained officers and men, and the folly of the administration had done its worst to discourage enlistment. When the danger seemed nearest, many great landowners had interested themselves personally and with great success to obtain recruits; and among others Lord Ilchester and Lord Digby in Somerset had attracted some of the best material to be found in rural England, promising that the men so enlisted should not be required to serve outside the Kingdom.

Notwithstanding this pledge, however, these recruits were by order of the Ministry forcibly driven on board transports and shipped off to Gibraltar. Never was there more brutal and heartless instance of the ill-faith kept by a British Government towards the British soldier. Having thus checked the flow of recruits at home, the Ministry turned to Holland and asked for the troops which she was bound by treaty to furnish. The request was refused; whereupon a royal message was actually sent, March 23, to Parliament announcing that the king in the present peril had sent for his contingent of Hessian troops from Germany, for the defence of England. The message was received with murmurs in the Commons, as well it might be, but it was not opposed; and indeed the climax of disgrace was not yet reached.

Whether from desire to embarrass Newcastle or to pay court to the king, Lord George Sackville, an officer whom before long we shall know too well, expressed a preference for Hanoverians over Hessians, and proposed an address praying the king to bring over his own electoral troops. Pitt left his sickbed and came down, ill as he was, to the House, to appeal to the history of the past and to the pride of every Englishman against the motion; yet it was passed by a majority of nearly three to one. The Lords consented to join the Commons in this address, the king granted their prayer, and the result was that both Hanoverians and Hessians were imported to defend this poor Island that could not defend herself.

The next business brought before Parliament furnished new evidence of the general confusion of affairs. As might have been foreseen, Frederick of Prussia had viewed with no friendly eye the treaty made by King George with Russia; and he now proposed, as an alternative, that Hanover and England should combine with Prussia to keep all troops whatsoever from entering the German Empire. Since Frederick had already announced his intention of attacking the Russians if they moved across the frontier, and since there was good reason to apprehend that, if driven to desperation, he might join with the French in overrunning Hanover, the Russian treaty was thrown over, and the new arrangement accepted by King George, Jan. 16. The pecuniary conditions attached to the agreement were duly ratified by the House of Commons in May, with results that were to reach further than were yet dreamed of. Then at last, apparently as an after-thought, war was formally declared. The country being thus definitely committed to a struggle which might be for life or death, the Lords supported by Newcastle seized the opportunity to reject the Militia Bill, which was the one important military measure so far brought forward. The general helplessness of the moment, owing to the absence of a strong hand at the helm, is almost incredible.

Meanwhile the French had struck their first blow, not on the shores of Britain, but at Minorca. As early as in January the Ministry had received good intelligence of the true destination of the enemy's armaments, but had made no sufficient preparation to meet the danger; nor was it until the 7th of April that it sent a fleet of ten ships, ill -manned and ill-found, under Admiral Byng to the Mediterranean. On the day following April 8, Byng's departure twelve ships of the line under M. de la Galissonière, with transports containing sixteen thousand troops under the Duke of Richelieu, weighed from Toulon, and on the 18th dropped anchor off the port of Ciudadella, at the north-western end of Minorca.

General Blakeney, the governor, had received warning of the intended attack two days before, and had made such preparations as he could for defence; but the means at his disposal were but poor. He had four regiments, the Fourth, Twenty-Third, Twenty-Fourth, and Thirty-Fourth of the Line; to which Commodore Edgcumbe, who was lying off Mahon with a squadron too weak to encounter the French, had added all the marines that he could spare before sailing away to Gibraltar. Even so, however, Blakeney could muster little more than twenty-eight hundred men.

But his most serious difficulty was lack of officers. He himself had won his ensigncy under Cutts the Salamander at Venloo, and he had maintained his reputation for firmness and courage at Stirling in 1745, but he was now past eighty, crippled with gout and unfit to bear the incessant labours of a siege. Nevertheless he was obliged to take the burden upon him from sheer dearth of senior officers. The lieutenant-governor of the Island, the governor of its principal defence, Fort Philip, and the colonels of all four regiments were absent; nineteen subalterns had never yet joined their respective corps, and nine more officers were absent on recruiting duties. In all five-and-thirty officers were wanting at their posts. It was the old evil against which George the First had struggled in vain, and it was now about to bear bitter fruit.

Richelieu landed on the 18th, and Blakeney at once withdrew the whole of his force to Fort St. Philip in order to make his stand there. This fortress, which commanded the town and harbour of Mahon, was probably the most elaborate possessed by the British, and was inferior in strength to few strongholds in Europe. Apart from the ordinary elaborations of the school of Vauban, it was strengthened by countless mines and galleries hewn out of the solid rock, which afforded unusual protection to the defenders. Blakeney had little time to break up the roads or otherwise to hinder the French advance; and Richelieu, marching into the town of Mahon on the 19th, was able a few days later to begin the siege. His operations, however, were unskilfully conducted, and the garrison defended itself with great spirit. An officer of engineers, Major Cunningham by name, while on his way to England from Minorca on leave, had heard of the French designs upon the Island and had instantly hurried back to his old post to assist in the defence; and his skill and resource were of inestimable value. So clumsily in fact did the French manage their operations that it was not until the 8th of May that their batteries began to May. produce the slightest effect.

Byng meanwhile had arrived at Gibraltar and had learned what was going forward. He carried the Seventh Fusiliers on board his fleet for Minorca, and had orders to embark yet another battalion from Gibraltar as a further reinforcement. General Fowke, however, who was in command at the Rock, urged that his instructions on this latter point were discretionary only and that he could not spare a battalion, having barely sufficient men to furnish reliefs for the ordinary guards. He therefore declined to grant more than two hundred and fifty men, to replace the marines landed from the fleet by Commodore Edgcumbe. It is instructive to note the difficulties imposed upon the commanders by the neglect of the government. Hitherto one of the first measures taken in prospect of a war had been the reinforcement of the Mediterranean garrisons. Now, after a full year of warning, they were left unstrengthened and unsupported. Nay, Richelieu had lain in front of Fort St. Philip for three whole weeks before three battalions were at last ordered to sail for Gibraltar, the 53rd, 54th and 57th, (*Secretary's Common Letter Book*, 12th May 1756).

Byng's fleet was so slenderly manned that he required the Seventh Fusiliers for duty on board ship, and therefore asked Fowke for a battalion for Minorca; Fowke's position was so weak that he dared not comply; and Blakeney's force was so inadequate that, though he could indeed hold his own in the fortress, he dared not venture his troops in a sortie. At length on the 19th of May Byng came in sight of Fort St. Philip, and on the following day fought the indecisive action and made the unfortunate retreat which became memorable through his subsequent fate.

The besieged, though greatly disappointed by his withdrawal, still defended themselves stoutly and with fine spirit. The fortress was well stored and the batteries were well and effectively served. Six more battalions were now sent to Richelieu, and the French plan of attack was altered. New batteries were built, which on the 6th of June opened fire from over one hundred guns and mortars, inflicting much damage and making a considerable breach. The British repaired the injured works and stood to their guns as steadily as ever; but on the 9th the French fire reopened more hotly than before and battered two new breaches.

Matters were now growing serious; and on the 14th a party of the garrison made a sally, drove the French from several of their batteries and spiked the guns, but pursuing their success too far were surrounded and captured almost to a man. Still Richelieu hesitated to storm; nor was it until the night of the 27th that he nerved himself for a final effort and made a grand attack upon several quarters of the fortress simultaneously. The defence was of the stubbornest, and the successful explosion of a mine sent three companies of French grenadiers flying into the air; but three of the principal outworks were carried, and the ablest officer of the garrison, Lieutenant Colonel Jefferies, while hurrying down to save one of them, was cut off and made prisoner with a hundred of his men.

Cunningham also was severely wounded and rendered unfit for duty. With hardly men enough left to him to man the guns, Blakeney on the 28th capitulated with the honours of war, and the garrison was embarked for Gibraltar. The siege had lasted for seventy days and had cost the French at the least two thousand men. The losses of the garrison were relatively small, amounting to less than four hundred killed and wounded, and the surrender was no dishonour to the British Army; but there was no disguising the disgraceful fact that Minorca was gone.

On the 14th of July the news reached England, and the nation, frantic with rage and shame, looked about savagely for a scapegoat. Bitter and cruel attacks were made even upon poor old Blakeney, who for all his fourscore years had never changed his clothes nor gone to bed during the ten weeks of the siege. Fowke was tried by court-martial for disobedience of orders in refusing to send the battalion required of him from Gibraltar, and though acquitted of all but an error in judgment and sentenced to a year's suspension only, was dismissed the service by the king. Finally, as is well known, the public indignation fastened itself upon Byng; and the unfortunate Admiral was shot because Newcastle deserved to be hanged. Old Blakeney alone, as was his desert, became a hero and was rewarded with an Irish peerage. Amid all the disgrace of that miserable time men found leisure to chronicle with a sneer that the veteran went to Court in a hackney coach with a foot-soldier behind it. St. James's would not have been the worse for a few more courtiers and lacqueys of the same rugged stamp.

More disasters were at hand; but the general paralysis in England continued. Such troops as the country possessed were still distributed as though an invasion were imminent. There was a camp at Cheltenham under Lord George Sackville, and another in Dorsetshire; the Hessians were at Winchester, the Hanoverians about Maidstone, the artillery massed together under the Duke of Marlborough at Byfleet; all doing nothing when there was so much to be done. The news of Braddock's defeat was nearly eight months old when Byng sailed for the Mediterranean.

The news of reverses in America heaped fuel on the flame of the nation's indignation against Newcastle; but meanwhile the cloud of war which had hung so long in menace over Europe burst at last in one tremendous storm. For some months past a league had been forming between France, Austria, Saxony, Russia, and Sweden to crush Frederick the Great and partition Prussia. France had been launched into this strange alliance by Madame de Pompadour, in revenge for Frederick's disdainful rejection of a friendly message; the *czarina* likewise sought vengeance for an epigram; Austria burned to recover Silesia; Saxony had been enticed by Austria with the lure of a share in partitioned Prussia; and Sweden had been attracted by the bait of Pomerania. Frederick, fully aware of all that was going forward, resolved to meet the danger rather than await it, and boldly invading Saxony began the Seven Years' War. Where it should end no man could divine.

All that was certain was that Frederick, far from protecting Hanover, would have much ado to defend himself. Thus, then, on the one side there was Hanover open to attack, and on the other Minorca lost, British naval reputation tarnished, and France triumphant in America. Further, though as yet men knew it not, the news of the loss of Calcutta and of the tragedy of the Black Hole was even then on its way across the ocean. The outcry against the government rose to a dangerous height; Fox deserted Newcastle, and resigned; and at length, in November, the shifty old jobber himself, after endless intrigues to retain office, reluctantly and ungracefully made way, nominally for the Duke of Devonshire, but in reality for William Pitt.

On the 2nd of December Parliament met, and the spirit of the new minister showed itself at once in the speech from the throne. The electoral troops and Hessians were to be sent back forthwith to Germany; and it was now the royal desire, which it had not been before Pitt took office, that the militia should be made more efficient. In a word, England was from henceforth to fight her battles for herself. Two days later leave was granted for the introduction of a Militia Bill, and on the 15th estimates were submitted for a British Establishment of thirty thousand men for the service of Great Britain and nineteen thousand for the colonies, besides two thousand artillery and engineers; the absence of Minorca from its usual place in the list of garrisons providing a significant comment on the whole.

Of the additional troops fifteen thousand had already been appointed for enlistment in September, when orders had been issued for the raising of a second battalion to each of fifteen regiments of the Line, (Miscellaneous Orders, 20th Sept. 1756). The regiments thus augmented were as follows, the regiments made from their second battalions being added in brackets. 3rd (61st), 4th (62nd), 8th (63rd), 11th (64th), 12th (65th), 19th (66th), 20th (67th), 23rd (68th), 24th (69th), 31st (70th), 32nd, 33rd, 34th, 36th, 37th.

These battalions were erected two years later into distinct regiments, of which ten still remain with us, numbered the Sixty-First to the Seventieth. This addition showed marks of Pitt's influence, but after the Christmas recess his handiwork was seen in a new and daring experiment, namely the formation of two regiments of Highlanders, each eleven hundred strong, which, though afterwards disbanded, became famous under the names of their colonels, Fraser and Montgomery, (*Miscellaneous Orders*, 4th Jan. 1757). The idea was a bold one, for it struck the last weapon from the dying hands of Jacobitism and turned it against itself; and the result soon approved it as a success. The existing Scottish regiments were required to contribute eighty non-commissioned officers who could speak Gaelic; and the Highlander from henceforth took his place not as a subverter of thrones but as a builder of empires. It is remarkable, concurrently, to note the sudden wave of energy which swept over the entire military administration in the first weeks of 1757, when the breath of one great man had once broken the springs and set the stagnant waters aflow.

Shirley's and Pepperrell's regiments, which had been crippled and ruined at Oswego, were struck off the list of the army to make room for more efficient corps. Newcastle's feeble ministers had directed the embarkation of a single battalion only, besides drafts, to America: Pitt, without counter-ordering these, ordered the augmentation and despatch of seven battalions more. The regiments were the 2nd batt. 1st Foot, 17th, 27th, 28th, 43rd, 46th, 55th Foot. The Forty-Ninth regiment, which was serving in Jamaica, was increased to nearly double of its former strength, to hearten the colonists in that Island. The Royal Artillery was raised to a total of twenty-four companies and distributed into two battalions, and a company of Miners, first conceived of six months before, was incorporated with it, (*Warrant Book*, 1st May 1756, 4th March 1757).

Finally, the Marines, which had been creeping up in strength ever since the beginning of the war, were augmented from one hundred to one hundred and thirty companies, so that men should not be lacking for the fleet. Nor was it only in the mere activity of departments and ubiquity of recruiting sergeants that the spirit of the master was seen. The nation was stirred by such military ardour as it had not felt since the Civil War, and there was a rush for commissions in the army, (so I gather from the countless letters on the subject in *Secretary's Common Letter Book,* Jan. and Feb. 1757).

On the re-assembling of Parliament the Militia Bill was again brought forward, and, though it did not pass the Lords until June, was so essential a feature of Pitt's first short administration that it may be dealt with here once and for all. The measure was introduced by George Townsend and was practically identical with that which had been rejected in the previous year, though Henry Conway, an officer of some distinction, had prepared an alternative scheme which was preferred by many. The bill as ultimately passed appointed a proportion of men to be furnished for the Militia in every county of England and Wales, from Devonshire and Middlesex, which were to provide sixteen hundred men apiece, to Anglesey, which was called upon for no more than eighty. These men were to be chosen by lot from lists drawn up by the parochial authorities for the Lords-Lieutenants and their deputies; and every man so chosen was to serve for three years, at the close of which period he was to enjoy exemption until his time should come again.

Thus it was designed that every eligible man in succession should pass through the ranks and serve for a fixed term. Special powers were given to justices and to deputy-lieutenants to discharge men from duty on sufficient reason shown, or after two years of service if they were over five-and-thirty years of age. The possession of a certain property was required as a qualification for officers, who likewise were entitled to discharge after four years' service, provided that others could be found to take their places. Provision was also made for the appointment by the king of an adjutant from the regular army to every regiment, and of a sergeant to every twenty men. The organisation was by regiments of from seven to twelve companies, in which no company was to be of smaller strength than eighty men. The Lord-Lieutenant of each county was in command of that county's militia; and in case of urgent danger the king was empowered to embody the whole force, communicating his reasons to Parliament if in session, when officers and men became entitled to the pay of their rank in the army and subject to the articles of war.

It had been part of the original design, favoured with reservations by Pitt himself, that Sunday should be a day of exercise, as in Switzerland and other Protestant countries; but this clause was dropped in deference to petitions from several dissenting sects, and it was finally enacted that the men should be drilled in half-companies and whole companies alternately on every Monday from April to October. The act was not passed without much opposition in the Lords, who indeed reduced the numbers of the force to thirty-two thousand men, or one-half of the strength voted by the Commons, and added clauses which clogged the working of the measure. Nor was it at first enforced without dangerous riot and tumult in some quarters, due principally to the unscrupulous employment, already narrated, of men enlisted for duty at home on foreign service. Nevertheless the great step was taken. A local force had been established for domestic defence, and the regular army was set free for service abroad, or more truly for the service of conquest.

During the early debates on the Militia Bill Pitt himself was absent, being confined to his house by gout; nor was it until the 17th of February that he appeared in his place to support the royal request for subsidies for Hanover and for the King of Prussia. The occasion drew upon him not a few sarcasms, for no man had more vehemently denounced the turning of Great Britain into a milch cow for the Electorate; but he waived the sneers aside in his wonted imperious fashion, for, consistent or inconsistent, he knew at least his own mind. It was one thing for British interests to be subordinated to Hanoverian; but it was quite another for Britain and Hanover to march shoulder to shoulder against a common enemy for their common advantage. The conquest of America in Germany was, as shall be seen, no idle phrase, though few as yet might comprehend its purport. But suddenly at this point Pitt's career was for the moment checked. Notwithstanding this proof of his loyalty to the cause of Hanover, the king was still unfriendly towards his new minister, and actually found, in the peril which threatened his beloved Electorate, a pretext for dismissing him from office.

In March 1757 a French army of one hundred thousand men poured over the Rhine; and it was necessary to call out the Hanoverian troops to oppose it. The king was urgent for the Duke of Cumberland to command these forces, but the duke was by no means so anxious to accept the trust. The memory of past failure oppressed him; and, since he hated Pitt, he was unwilling to correspond with him or to depend on him for instructions and supplies. To obviate this difficulty the king agreed to remove Pitt; and thus a minister of genius was discarded that an unskilful commander might take the field. It was a proceeding worthier of Versailles than of St. James's.

On the 5th of April Pitt, having refused to resign, received intimation of his dismissal; but by this time the nation had been roused to such a pitch that it would suffer no return to the imbecile and disgraceful administration of the past two years. The stocks fell; all the principal towns in England sent the freedom of their corporations to Pitt, and, in Walpole's phrase, for weeks it rained gold boxes. The king turned to Newcastle, but the contemptible old intriguer tried in vain to form a government with Pitt or without him. For eleven whole weeks the negotiations continued and the country was left virtually without a government of any kind, until at length it was seen that Pitt's return to office was inevitable, and on the 27th of July, though Newcastle still retained the post of First Lord of the Treasury, Pitt was finally reinstated as Secretary of State on his own terms, that is to say, with full control of the war and of foreign affairs. "I will borrow the duke's majority to carry on the government," he had said, "I am sure that I can save this country and that no one else can."

The king's perversity in driving Pitt from office had brought speedy judgment upon himself and upon Cumberland. The duke was defeated by the French at the Battle of Hastenbeck, July 26, and retreating upon Stade concluded, or rather found concluded for him, the convention of Klosterzeven, Sept 5, whereby he agreed to evacuate the country. Such were the discouragements which confronted Pitt on resuming office. It was hard to see how he could initiate any operations of value at so late a period of the year, but there was one species of diversion which, though little recommended by experience of the past, lay open to him still, namely a descent upon the French coast.

A young Scottish officer, who had travelled in France, gave intelligence based on no very careful or recent observation, that the fortifications of Rochefort were easily assailable; and Pitt on the receipt of this intelligence at once conceived the design of surprising Rochefort and burning the ships in the Charente below it. Somewhat hastily it was determined to send ten of the best battalions and a powerful fleet on this enterprise, and the military command was offered to Lord George Sackville, who not relishing the task found an excuse for declining. Pitt was then for entrusting it to General Henry Conway, but the king objected to this officer on the score of his youth, and insisted on setting over him Sir John Mordaunt, a veteran who had showed merit in the past, but had now lost his nerve and was conscious that he had lost it. He and Conway alike objected to the project as based on flimsy and insufficient information, but both thought themselves bound in honour to accept the trust confided to them.

Though the expedition had been decided upon in July, it was not until two months later that it sailed from England, and meanwhile the troops waited as usual in the Isle of Wight. The regiments were the 3rd, 5th, 8th, 15th, 20th, 24th, 25th, 30th, 50th, 51st. There was much delay in providing transports, and the embarkation was so ill-managed that the troops were obliged to row a full mile to their ships. On the 8th of September, however, the vessels put to sea under convoy of sixteen sail of the line under Sir Edward Hawke, and after much delay from foul winds and calms anchored in Basque Roads, the haven which was to become famous half a century later for an attack of a very different kind.

On the 23rd the fortifications of the Isle d'Aix were battered down by the fleet and the island itself captured; but therewith the operations came abruptly to an end. Fresh information revealed that the French were fully prepared to meet an attack on Rochefort; and a council of war decided that any attempt to take it by escalade would be hopeless. It was therefore decided to attack the forts at the mouth of the Charente, but the order was countermanded by Mordaunt; and after a week's delay Hawke gave the general to understand that unless operations were prosecuted forthwith he would return with the fleet to England. The military commanders thereupon decided that they would return with him, which on the 1st of October they did, to the huge indignation of both fleet and army.

A court of inquiry was held over this absurd issue to such extensive and costly preparations, and Sir John Mordaunt was tried by court-martial but honourably acquitted. The incident gave rise to a fierce war of pamphlets. It is certain that Mordaunt showed remarkable supineness, and he was suspected of a wish to injure the influence of Pitt by turning the enterprise into ridicule; but with such men as Wolfe, Conway and Cornwallis among the senior officers, the only conclusion is that, in the view of military men, no object of the least value could have been gained by any operations whatever. Military opinion had been against the expedition from the first. Ligonier, a daring officer but of ripe experience and sound judgment, wrote of it in the most lukewarm terms as likely to lead to nothing. On the whole it seems that the troops were sent on a fool's errand, and that the blame lay solely with Pitt.

The nation was furious, and the king showed marked coldness towards the generals who had taken part in the failure; but Pitt, who was more hurt and disappointed than any one, took no step except to promote Wolfe, who had advocated active measures, over the heads of several other officers, and thus in one way at least extracted good from evil.

So ended the campaigning season of 1757 with an unbroken record of ill success in every quarter. But the right man was now at the head of affairs and was looking about J him for the right instruments. The long period of darkness had come to an end and the light was about to break, at first in flickering broken rays, but soon to shine out in one blaze of dazzling and surpassing splendour.

Pitt had now a free hand for the execution of such enterprises as he might desire, a freer hand indeed than any of his predecessors for ten years past had enjoyed; for Cumberland, being ill-received by the king on his return from Hastenbeck, had resigned the commandership-in-chief and all his military appointments of whatever description. Pitt, conscious that the duke had been hardly treated, made no secret of his sympathy with him; but there can be no doubt that Ligonier, who succeeded him as commander-in-chief, was infinitely more competent as a military adviser and more sympathetic as a military colleague. And there was need for sound military capacity to deal with all the projects that were ripening in the minister's teeming brain.

Parliament met on the 1st of December, and the king's speech, after announcing vigorous prosecution of the war in America and elsewhere, begged for support for the King of Prussia. Frederick fortunately stood just at that moment at his highest in the public view, for his two masterly victories at Rossbach and Leuthen; and Parliament did not hesitate to confirm a subsidy to him to enable him to carry on the struggle. But in other respects Pitt could find little to boast of in the past year, and he was obliged to confine his eulogy to Frederick and to Clive, whose victory at Plassey, June 23, now just become known in England, could not be ascribed to any extraordinary efforts on the part of a British Ministry. The word "elsewhere" in the king's speech was understood to signify Hanover, though Pitt warmly disclaimed any such interpretation of the term; but the Commons did not quarrel with it nor with the estimates that were submitted in support of the policy.

These were presented on the 7th of December and showed a

force for the British Establishment of eighty-six thousand five hundred men, thirty thousand of them for Gibraltar and the colonies, and the remainder nominally for service at home. Four thousand of this number, however, were invalids, who were kept for duties in garrison only, a system wisely copied from earlier days and followed from the beginning to the end of the war. One new regiment only had been raised since the formation of Fraser's and Montgomery's Highlanders, namely Colonel Draper's, which had been created for service in India and which brought up the number of the regiments of the Line to seventy-nine. Adding the troops on the Irish to those on the British Establishment the full numbers of the army may be set down roughly at one hundred thousand men. It was soon to be seen what Pitt could accomplish with them, when he had found officers who would fulfil his instructions.

CHAPTER 6

The French Raids

The French colonies during the Seven Year's War were allowed to take their chance, while French soldiers were poured by the hundred thousand into Germany to avenge King Frederick's sarcasm against Madame de Pompadour. A Pitt was hardly needed to perceive that the more employment that could be found for French armies in Europe, the fewer were the men which could be spared for the service of France's possessions beyond sea; and Pitt resolved accordingly to keep those armies fully occupied. By the convention of Klosterzeven it was agreed that the Hanoverian army should be broken up; but even before Cumberland's return to England, the question of repudiating that convention had been broached, and a fortnight later a message was despatched to Frederick announcing that the army would take the field again, and requesting the services of Prince Ferdinand of Brunswick as General-in-Chief.

Frederick assented; and on the 24th of November, 1757, Ferdinand arrived at Stade, fresh from the victory of Rossbach in which he had taken part three weeks before, to assume the command. The whole aspect of affairs changed instantly, as if by magic. Setting his force in motion at once Ferdinand by the end of the year had driven the French back to the Aller, (Feb. 15th, 1758),and renewing operations after six weeks spent in winter-quarters pressed the enemy still farther back, even across the Rhine.

It is said that even before Ferdinand had achieved this success Pitt had resolved to reinforce him with British troops, but for the present the minister reverted to his old plan of a descent on the French coast, which might serve the purpose of diverting French troops alike from America and from Germany. The first sign of his intention was seen in April 1758, when the officers of sixteen battalions received orders to repair to the Isle of Wight by the middle of May. Such long notice was a strange preliminary for a secret expedition, for the troops themselves did not receive their orders until the 20th of May; and it was the end of the month before the whole of them, some thirteen thousand men,[1] were encamped on the island. The Duke of Marlborough was selected for the command, and, since his military talent was doubtful, Lord George Sackville, whose ability was unquestioned, was appointed as his second, with the duty of organising the whole of the operations.

Two squadrons, comprising twenty-four ships of the line under Lord Anson, Sir Edward Hawke, and Commodore Howe, were detailed to escort the transports, and on the 1st of June the armament set sail, arriving on the 5th at Cancalle Bay, about eight miles from St. Malo. A French battery, erected for the defence of the bay, was quickly silenced by the ships, and on the following day the entire army was landed. One brigade was left to guard the landing-place, and the remainder of the force marched to St. Malo, where the light dragoons under cover of night slipped down to the harbour and burned over a hundred privateers and merchant-vessels.

The Duke of Marlborough then made dispositions as if for the siege of St. Malo, but hearing that a superior force was on the march to cut off his retreat, retired to Cancalle Bay, re-embarked the troops, and sailed against Granville, a petty town some twenty miles to northeast of St. Malo. Foul weather frustrated the intended operations; and on the 27th the expedition arrived off Havre de Grace. Preparations were made for landing, but after two days of inactivity Marlborough decided against an attack, and the fleet bore up for Cherbourg.

There once more all was made ready for disembarkation, but the weather was adverse, forage and provisions began to fail, and the entire enterprise against the coast was abandoned. So the costly armament returned to Portsmouth, (July 1st), having effected absolutely nothing. It is, however, doubtful whether blame can be attached to the officers, either naval or military, for the failure. Pitt had procured no intelligence as to the dispositions of the French for defence of the threatened ports; so that a general might well hesitate to run the risk of landing, when he could not tell how soon he might find himself cut off by a superior force from the sea.

---

1. The troops were, one battalion from each regiment of Guards, the 5th, 8th, 20th, 23rd, 24th, 25th, 30th, 33rd, 34th, and 36th Foot; the light troops of nine dragoon regiments, three companies of artillery and a large siege-train.

Meanwhile Ferdinand following up his success had pursued the French over the Rhine and gained a signal victory over them at Creveld. This action appears to have hastened Pitt to a decision, for within four days he announced to the British Commissary at Ferdinand's headquarters the king's intention to reinforce the prince with two thousand British cavalry. The troops were warned for service on the same day; but within three days it was decided to increase the reinforcement to six thousand troops, both horse and foot, and a week later the force was further augmented by three battalions. The first division of the troops was shipped off to Emden on the 11th of July, and by the second week in August the entire reinforcement had disembarked at the same port under command of the Duke of Marlborough, joining Prince Ferdinand's army at Coesfeld on the 21st. [2] There for the present we must leave them, till the time comes for Ferdinand's operations to engage our whole attention. Meanwhile the reader need bear in mind only that the British Army is definitely committed to yet another theatre of war.

Even so, however, Pitt remained unsatisfied without another stroke against the French coast. While the troops were embarking for Germany he had formed a new encampment on the Isle of Wight and was intent upon a raid on Cherbourg. So intensely distasteful were these expeditions to the officers of the Army that the Duke of Marlborough and Lord George Sackville used their interest to obtain appointment to the army in Germany, so as to be quit of them once for all. The result was that when Lieutenant-General Bligh, who had been originally selected to serve under Prince Ferdinand, arrived in London from Ireland to sail for Emden, he found to his dismay that his destination was changed, and that he must prepare to embark for France. He accepted the command as in duty bound, the more so since Prince Edward was to accompany the expedition, but he was little fit for the service, having no qualification except personal bravery and one great disqualification in advanced age. Accordingly, obedient but unwilling, he set sail on the 1st of August with twelve battalions [3] and nine troops of light dragoons, escorted by a squadron under Commodore Howe. Not yet had the gallant sailor learned of his succession to the

---

2 The troops were, the Blues, 1st and 3rd Dragoon Guards, Greys, Inniskillings, 10th Dragoons (now Hussars), 12th, 20th, 25th, 37th, 51st Foot, with one battalion of Invalids to garrison Emden.
3. Three battalions of Guards, the 5th, 24th, 30th, 33rd, 34th, 36th, 67th, 68th, and the Duke of Richmond's Foot (then numbered 72nd).

title through the fall of his brother Lord Howe at the head of Lake Champlain.

The expedition began prosperously enough. The fleet arrived before Cherbourg on the 6th and at once opened the bombardment of the town. Early next morning it sailed to the bay of St. Marais, two leagues from Cherbourg, where the Guards and the grenadier companies, having landed under the fire of the ships, attacked and drove off a force of three thousand French which had been drawn up to oppose them. The rest of the troops disembarked without hindrance on the following day and advanced on Cherbourg, which being unfortified to landward surrendered at once. Bligh thereupon proceeded to destroy the docks and the defences of the harbour and to burn the shipping, while the light cavalry scoured the surrounding country and levied contributions. This done, the troops were re-embarked; and after long delay owing to foul winds the fleet came to anchor on the 3rd of September in the Bay of St. Lunaire, some twelve miles east of St. Malo.

There the troops were again landed during the two following days, though not without difficulty and the loss of several men drowned. Bligh's instructions bade him carry on operations against Morlaix or any other point on the coast that he might prefer to it, and he had formed some vague design of storming St. Malo from the landward side. This, however, was found to be impracticable with the force at his disposal; and now there ensued an awkward complication. The weather grew steadily worse, and Howe was obliged to warn the General that the fleet must leave the dangerous anchorage at St. Lunaire, and that it would be impossible for him to re-embark the troops at any point nearer than the bay of St. Cast, a few miles to westward. Accordingly he sailed for St. Cast, while Bligh, now thrown absolutely on his own resources ashore, marched for the same destination overland.

The army set out on the morning of the 7th of September, and after some trouble with small parties of French on the march encamped on the same evening near the River Equernon, intending to ford it next morning. It speaks volumes for the incapacity of Bligh and of his staff that the passage of the river was actually fixed for six o'clock in the morning, though that was the hour of high water. It was of course necessary to wait for the ebb-tide; so it was not until three in the afternoon that the troops forded the river, even then waist-deep, under a brisk fire from small parties of French peasants and regular troops. Owing to the lateness of the hour further advance on that day

86

was impossible; and on resuming the march on the following morning the advanced guard encountered a body of about five hundred French troops. The enemy were driven back with considerable loss, but their prisoners gave information of the advance of at least ten thousand French from Brest. Arrived at Matignon Bligh encamped and sent his engineers to reconnoitre the beach at St. Cast in case he should be compelled to retreat. Deserters who came in during the night reported that the French were gathering additional forces from the adjacent garrisons; and in the morning Bligh sent word to Howe that he intended to embark on the following day.

Constant alarms during the night showed that the enemy was near at hand; and it would have been thought that Bligh, having made up his mind to retreat, would in so critical a position have retired as swiftly and silently as possible. On the contrary, at three o'clock on the morning of the 11th the drums beat the assembly as usual, to give the French all the information that they desired; while the troops moved off in a single column so as to consume the longest possible time on the march. It was nine o'clock before the embarkation began, and at eleven, when two-thirds of the force had been shipped, the enemy appeared in force on the hills above the beach. For some time the French were kept at a distance by the guns of the fleet, but after an hour they found shelter and opened a sharp and destructive fire.

General Drury, who commanded the rear-guard, consisting of fourteen hundred men of the Guards and the grenadiers, was obliged to form his men across the beach to cover the embarkation. Twice he drove back the enemy, but, ammunition failing, he was forced back in turn, and there was nothing left but a rush for the boats. The French bringing up their artillery opened a furious fire; and all was confusion. So many of the boats were destroyed that the sailors shrank from approaching the shore and were only kept to their work by the personal example of Howe. In all seven hundred and fifty officers and men were killed and wounded, General Drury being among the slain, and the rest of the rearguard were taken prisoners. The fleet and transports made their way back to England in no comfortable frame of mind, for the French naturally magnified their success to the utmost; and so ended Pitt's third venture against the coast of France.

There can be little doubt but that Bligh must be held responsible for the failure. It should seem indeed that he was ignorant of the elements of his duty, even to the enforcing of discipline among the troops, who at the first landing near Cherbourg behaved disgracefully.

The Duke of Marlborough had met with the same trouble at Cancalle Bay, but had had at least the strength to hang a marauding soldier on the first day and so to restore order. But after all Pitt was presumably responsible for the selection of Bligh; or, if he was aware that he could not appoint the right man for such a service, he would have done better to abandon these raids on the French coast altogether. The conduct of Marlborough and Sackville in shirking the duty because it was distasteful to them does not appear commendable; but Sackville at any rate was no fool, and Pitt might at least have recognised the military objections that were raised against his plans.

The truth of the matter is, as Lord Cochrane was to prove fifty years later, that sporadic attacks on the French coast are best left to the navy; for a single frigate under a daring and resolute officer can paralyse more troops than an expedition of ten or fifteen thousand men, with infinitely less risk and expense. Pitt had not yet done with his favourite descents, but his next venture of the kind was to be directed against an island instead of the mainland, when the British fleet could interpose between his handful of battalions and the whole population of France. Meanwhile Cherbourg had at any rate been destroyed, so like a wise man the minister made the most of this success, by sending some of the captured guns with great parade through Hyde Park to the Tower.

The operations of the year 1758 were of considerable scope, embracing as they did the advance of three separate armies in America, two raids on the French coast, and the despatch of British troops to Germany; but these by no means exhaust the tale. There were few quarters of the globe in which the British had not to complain of French encroachment, and to this insidious hostility Pitt had resolved to put a stop once for all.

CHAPTER 7

The Battle of Minden

In the spring of 1759 ten thousand British troops were about to enter on their first campaign under Prince Ferdinand of Brunswick. Yet it never occurred to Pitt to recall one man of them, notwithstanding the peril of invasion. It may be asked why the ten thousand, being so near home, were not summoned from Germany, and of what possible service they could have been on the Continent. Pitt spoke but half the truth when he spoke of conquering America in Germany; it was not only America, but the East and West Indies, in a word the British Empire. The war in Germany was in fact nothing more than a diversion on a grand scale, and it is as such that it must now be followed. The French likewise pursued their idea of a diversion when they threatened a descent upon the shores of Great Britain. It was a plan which they had employed with some success in the days of King William and of Queen Anne, but it had not saved them from Marlborough at Oudenarde, and it was not to deliver them from the busy designs of Pitt.

Before entering on the campaigns of Prince Ferdinand it is indispensable to attempt to grasp the general purport of the operations on either side. The French had invaded Germany primarily to take vengeance upon Prussia for King Frederick's scornful treatment of Madame de Pompadour. Frederick, being already occupied with the Saxons and Austrians to the south and with the Russians on his flank to the eastward, could hardly have escaped disaster with the French pressing on his other flank from the west. He had indeed, in 1758, with the swiftness that characterised his operations, made a dash upon the French and hurled them back at Rossbach, and within a month dealt the Austrians as severe a buffet at Leuthen with the same army. But to defeat two armies at two points over two hundred miles apart within a few weeks, was a strain that could not be repeated; and it was

Ferdinand of Brunswick

primarily to guard Frederick's right or western flank that Ferdinand's army was called into being. So far as Frederick was concerned it quite fulfilled its purpose; but in the eyes of England its mission was somewhat different.

Under the Duke of Cumberland the force had been called an army of observation, to secure the frontiers of Hanover; and Cumberland, despite Frederick's warnings, had endeavoured to cover Hanover by holding the line of the Weser, with results that were seen at Hastenbeck. Under Ferdinand the army became an Allied Army for active operations in concert with King Frederick; but none the less its chief function was to cover Hanover, Hesse-Cassel, and Brunswick. For the French army, being lax in discipline, behaved with shameful inhumanity towards the inhabitants of German territory during this war; and there was always apprehension lest the rulers of Hesse and Brunswick, from sheer compassion towards their suffering people, should withdraw from the Alliance.

Throughout the operations about to come under our notice the French acted with at least two armies, jointly superior to Ferdinand's in numbers, along two different lines. The northern army was known as the Army of the Rhine, its base being Wesel on the Lower Rhine, an outlying possession of King Frederick's, which had perforce been abandoned by him at the opening of the war, and which despite Ferdinand's efforts could never be recovered. This army was destined to advance into Westphalia, and thence, if possible, into Hanover; and a glance at the map will show that its simplest line of advance was by the River Lippe. The second or southern army of the French was known as the Army of the Main; having provided itself with a base on that river by the treacherous capture of Frankfort.[1]

This was one of the many unscrupulous actions whereby the French made themselves loathed in Europe; for Frankfort being an Imperial Free Town was held always to be neutral. Still the thing was done; and thereby was secured to the Army of the Main, which had begun life as the Army of the Upper Rhine, not only an excellent base but a sure means of retreat. For the Allies, even if they defeated it, could not bar its way to the Rhine until Frankfort should be first besieged and captured, which could not but be a very arduous undertaking. The primary function of this second army was the invasion of Hesse.

---

1. It is hardly necessary to recall to readers the story of the occupation of Frankfort in Goethe's *Dichtung und Wahrheit,*

Ferdinand's task, with an inferior force, was in its essence defensive. For him the supremely important thing was to retain possession of the line of the Weser, on which waterway he depended for his supplies alike from Germany and from England. Thus, roughly speaking, the field of operations lay between the Rhine on the one side and the Weser on the other, with the sea and the Main for northern and southern boundaries; and the normal front of the French would be to the east and of the Allies to the west. But it must be remembered that in addition to the army operating from Wesel against Ferdinand's front there was another operating from Frankfort upon his left or southern flank; while there was always the further danger that the Saxons might elude a Prussian corps of observation, which was posted to check them, on the south-east, and steal in upon Ferdinand's left rear.

To defeat these combinations it was of vital importance to Ferdinand to hold in particular two fortresses—Münster in Westphalia, since the French, if they took it, could push on unhindered to the Weser and cut off his supplies; and Lippstadt on the Upper Lippe, which secured communications between Münster and Cassel, or in other words between Westphalia and Hesse, and contrariwise impeded the joint action of the two French armies. For the rest it will be useful to take note of three rivers which barred the advance of the French northward from Frankfort to Cassel and beyond: namely, counting from south to north, the Ohm, the Eder, and the Diemel. With the last in particular, as the final barrier between Hesse and Westphalia, we shall have much to do; so the reader would do well to grasp its position once for all, not neglecting its relation to the neighbouring waters of the Lippe and the Weser.

At the close of the campaign of 1758 Ferdinand's winter quarters extended from Coesfeld, a little to westward of Münster, through Münster, Lippstadt and Paderborn to the Diemel, his front facing thus somewhat to south of south-east. The French Army of the Rhine under Marshal Contades was cantoned along that river from Wesel southward almost to Coblentz; while the army of the Main, under the Prince of Soubise, the defeated General of Rossbach, lay just to north of the river about Frankfort. Ferdinand's first trouble was with an advance of the Austrians upon his left flank by the River Werra. This he headed back by a rapid march to Fulda; and, being freed from this danger, he of resolved to turn this enforced movement to southward, to account by making a bold stroke upon Frankfort, so as, if possible, to paralyse the operations of the French on that side by snatching from them their base.

Unfortunately for him, the incapable Soubise had been recalled to command the army for invasion of England, and Marshal Broglie, who had succeeded him, had entrenched himself in a strong position at Bergen, a little to the north of Frankfort. There on the 13th of April, just five days after the storm of Masulipatam, Ferdinand boldly attacked him,[2] but was repulsed with a loss of over two thousand men, and compelled to fall back to Ziegenhain, on the road to Cassel. His audacious attempt to cripple one French Army, before the campaign had even been opened, had failed.

After this alarm the French employed themselves busily in entrenching themselves on the Main. Prince Henry of Prussia, by King Frederick's direction, marched northward to relieve Ferdinand from further trouble from the Austrians; and the enemy made little movement during the ensuing month. On the 25th of April Contades arrived at Düsseldorf from Paris with an approved plan of campaign in his pocket, and proceeded to distribute the army of the Rhine into four corps, two of them about Wesel, a third at Düsseldorf, and a fourth about Cologne. This grouping, as Contades intended, left Ferdinand in doubt whether his main design was aimed at Westphalia or Hesse. The corps which guarded Westphalia included the British contingent under Lord George Sackville, who had been appointed to the command on the death of the Duke of Marlborough in the previous year, and it lay a little to the west of Münster, under the orders of the Hanoverian General von Spörcke.

That officer growing uneasy over Contades's movements, Ferdinand on the 16th of May marched from Ziegenhain, leaving sixteen thousand men under General von Imhoff to protect Hesse, and on the 24th, having effected his junction with Spörcke, cantoned his troops along the Lippe from Coesfeld to Hamm. Meanwhile Contades, detaching a corps of fifteen thousand men under Count d'Armentières to threaten Münster, marched southward from Düsseldorf, on May 27th, upon Giessen, there to join Broglie and begin operations against Hesse. Ferdinand, in the faint hope of recalling him to the Rhine, despatched a corps under the Hereditary Prince of Brunswick, a most brilliant officer, to alarm the French garrisons at Düsseldorf and other points on the river; but Contades, adhering to his purpose, pushed forward, May 29th, an advanced corps under M. de Noailles from Giessen to Marburg, evidently intent on prosecuting his march to the north.

2. Some British squadrons were present at this action but were not engaged.

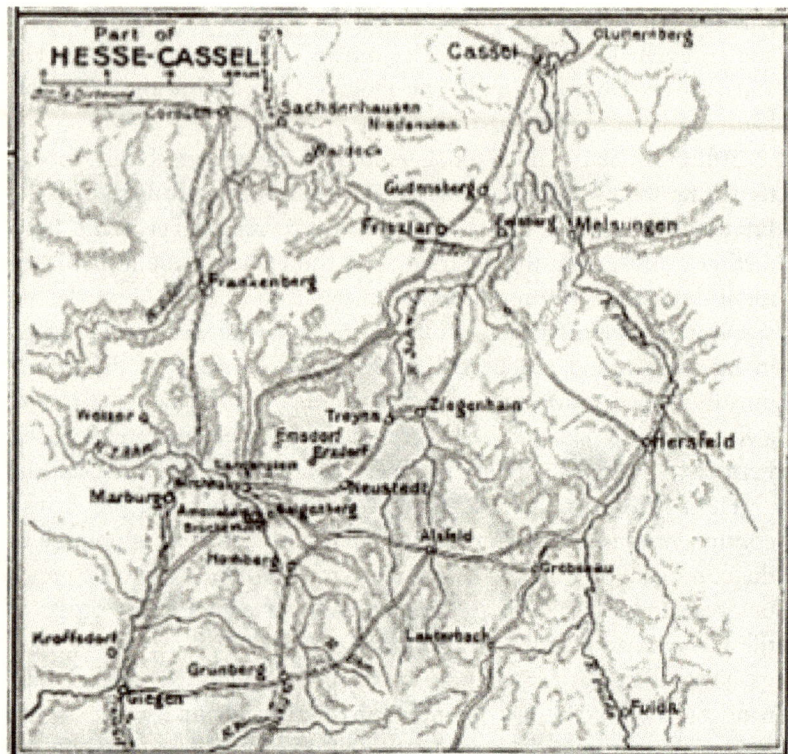

Part of
HESSE-CASSEL

Cassel

Gudensberg

Fritzlar

Melsungen

Frankenberg

Treysa

Ziegenhain

Hersfeld

Marburg

Neustadt

Homberg

Alsfeld

Grebenau

Grunberg

Lauterbach

Giessen

Fulda

Contades was in overwhelming force. Noailles's corps at Marburg numbered twenty thousand men, his own at Giessen close on sixty thousand, while Broglie's reserve-corps at Friedberg, a little to the south of Giessen, included close on twenty thousand more. He now sent Broglie forward by Fritzlar upon Cassel, while he himself continued his march due north through Waldeck upon Corbach. Imhoff, fearful of being cut off and unable to defend Cassel, fell back towards Lippstadt; and Broglie having left a force to occupy Cassel, turned westward to rejoin Contades. On the 14th of June the whole were again assembled together, Contades' corps lying a little to the south of Paderborn, and Broglie's at Stadtbergen.

These movements caused Ferdinand the deepest anxiety. On the 11th of June he concentrated and marched eastward to Büren, where he halted and picked up Imhoff's corps; but even so he was weaker than the enemy, for though he had recalled the hereditary prince from Düsseldorf, he had been obliged to leave nine thousand men under General Wangenheim at Dülmen, to watch d'Armentières's designs against Münster. But worse was to come; for on the 18th Broglie's corps, moving up to the right of Contades's, began to edge Ferdinand's left wing back to the westward. Ferdinand, accepting the inevitable, fell back on Lippstadt and crossed the Lippe to Rietberg. His embarrassment was now extreme. He could not divine whether the enemy designed to besiege Lippstadt or Münster or both, or whether they meant to force a battle upon him against greatly superior numbers. He was inclined to risk a battle, seeing that, for all that he could do to prevent it, both fortresses might be taken before his eyes; in which case he must needs cross to the east side of the Weser.

So critical did he consider the position that he wrote to King George the Second for instructions, and begged that ships might be ready to transport the garrison in case it should be necessary to evacuate Emden. The king's answer showed the Guelphic loyalty and courage at its noblest. He said that since Ferdinand was inclined to hazard an action he also was ready to take the risk, but that he left his general an absolutely free hand, only assuring him that his confidence in him would be unabated, whatever the result; and, lest Ferdinand should be in any doubt, he caused a second letter to be written to him to the same effect, but in stronger terms even than the first.

Meanwhile Contades marched up to Paderborn and halted for some days, keeping Ferdinand still in doubt as to his intentions. At last on the 29th he moved northward and pushed his light troops forward to Bielefeld, showing plainly that his true aim was the capture either of Hameln or of Minden on the Weser. Ferdinand therefore recalled Wangenheim's corps from Dülmen to the main army, July 3rd; whereupon, as he had expected, d'Armentières at once advanced to besiege Münster. On the same day Ferdinand himself moved northward and encamped parallel to Contades at Diessen, comforting himself with the reflection that though his enemies might be nearer to Minden than he, he at any rate was nearer to his food-supplies than they.

It was, however, extremely difficult for him to obtain intelligence of the French movements, since the two armies were separated by a broad chain of wooded hills; and he consequently hesitated for some days before he decided, on false information of a French advance, July 8th, to move towards Osnabrück.

His intention was to turn eastward from thence, and to take up a position which would render it perilous for the French to attempt the siege either of Hameln or Minden. He had made, however, but one march from Osnabrück when he received the news, July 10th, that Broglie had surprised Minden on the day before, and that the French had thus secured a bridge over the Weser and free access into Hanover. This was a most unpleasant surprise for Ferdinand. For a day he hesitated whether or not to return to Münster, and then decided to fall back to the Lower Weser, so as to save his magazine at Nienburg, and, since the French had set the example of lawlessness at Frankfort, to occupy the Imperial Free Town of Bremen. On the 14th of July accordingly his headquarters were fixed at Stolzenau, between Nienburg and Minden on the Weser, and a detachment was sent to Bremen.

Meanwhile Contades proceeded to reap the fruit of his very successful movements. Part of his light troops seized upon Osnabrück, and the rest were sent to levy contributions in Hanover; M. de Chevreuse was detached with three thousand men to besiege Lippstadt; d'Armentières continued to besiege Münster; Broglie's corps crossed the Weser on the 14th to invest Hameln; and on the 16th Contades with the main army debouched into the basin of Minden, and pushed a part of his army as far to the northward as Petershagen. Ferdinand, though he could bring but forty-five thousand men into the field against sixty thousand, advanced southward next day to offer him battle; but Contades retired without awaiting his arrival and withdrew to an unassailable position immediately to south of Minden. If he could hold Ferdinand inactive while his several detachments did their work, it was of no profit to him to hazard a general action.

So far Contades's operations had been masterly. He had taken Cassel, the capital of Hesse, and had invested both Lippstadt and Münster; he had further taken Minden and invested Hameln; and thus he bade fair to possess himself of the line of the Weser and to carry the war straight into Hanover. Ferdinand's position was most critical, and was not rendered more pleasant to him by a series of uncomplimentary messages from Frederick the Great. But Contades, from the moment that he declined battle, seems to have taken leave, possibly from excessive confidence, of all energy and ability. His position was, it is true, impregnable. His army lay immediately to the south of Minden, communicating by three bridges with Broglie's corps on the other side of the Weser. His right rested on the town and the river, his left on a mass of wooded hills—the end of the range that had separated his army from Ferdinand's—and the whole of his front was covered by a wide morass, through which ran a brook called the Bastau.

But though unassailable from any point, the position had conspicuous defects. In the first place, it did not leave the army free to move in all directions; and in the second, it necessitated the detachment of troops to the south to maintain communication through Gohfeld and Hervorden with the French base at Cassel. It was for Ferdinand, by skilful use of these defects, to entice Contades from his pinfold to meet him in the open field.

Returning to camp at Petershagen, (July), after Contades's withdrawal to Minden, Ferdinand's first step was to push his picquets forward into a chain of villages that lay in his front: Todtenhausen on the bank of the Weser, Fredewald immediately to west of Todtenhausen, Stemmern and Holthausen somewhat in advance of Fredewald, and Nord Hemmern, Sud Hemmern, and Hille still farther to south and west. The occupation of Hille brought his advanced posts to the western edge of the morass that covered Contades's front, and to the head of the one causeway that led across it. On the 22nd Wangenheim's corps, about ten thousand strong, was pushed forward to Todtenhausen, where it remained conspicuous, in advance of the army. In the midst of these movements came the bad news of the fall of Münster, which enabled d'Armentières to march from thence to besiege Lippstadt, and Chevreuse to return with his detachment to Minden; but this misfortune only quickened Ferdinand to action.

On the 27th the hereditary prince marched with six thousand men south-westward towards Lübbecke, and on the following day drove from it a body of French irregulars which was stationed there

MINDEN,

Aug. 1st 1759.

The Action at the moment of the attack of the British Infantry.

British
Allies
French

0   100   200   400 Yards.

VERD...

Hille

Hille...

Nor...

Sud Hammern

Hartum

R. Bastau

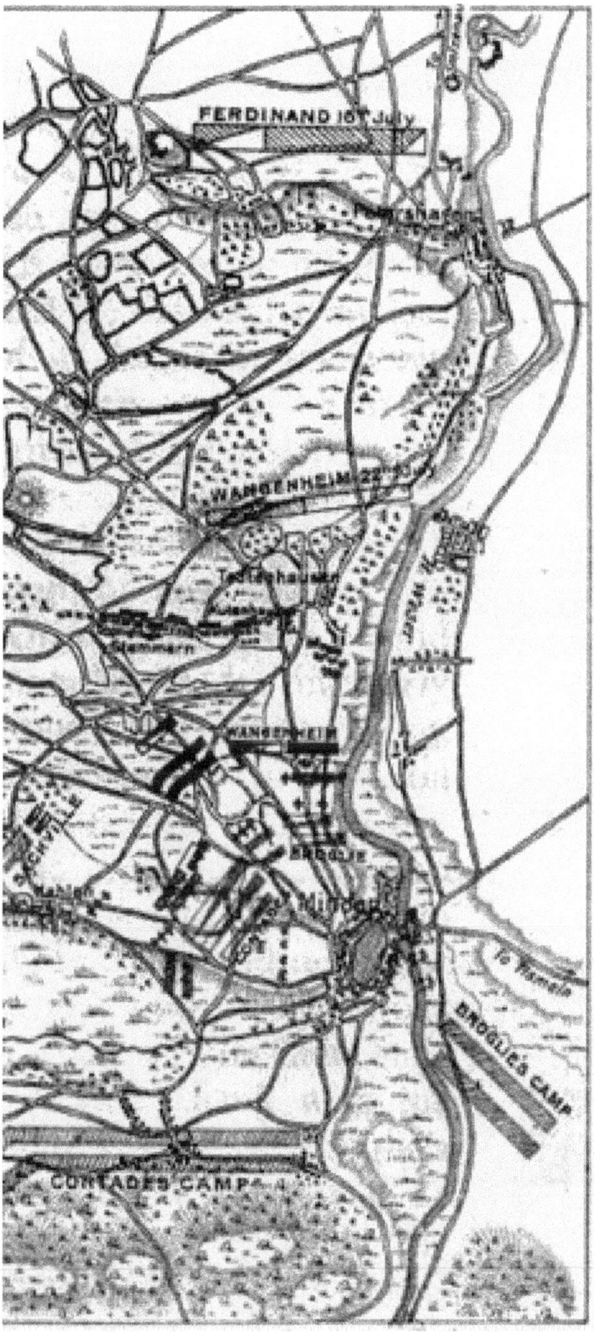
FERDINAND 16th July
WANGENHEIM
BROGLIE
Minden
To Hameln
BROGLIE'S CAMP
CONTADES CAMP

for the protection of Contades's left flank. Then turning eastward he pursued his march against the French communications. Simultaneously, on the 28th, General Dreve led the garrison of Bremen against Osnabrück, retook it, and hastened eastward to join the hereditary prince. The junction effected, the two pressed on towards Hervorden, and on the 31st established themselves astride of the road by which all Contades's supplies must be brought up from the south.

Here, therefore, was a menace in his rear to make the French general uneasy in his position behind the morass; and now Ferdinand added a temptation in his front to induce him the more readily to quit it. On the 29th the prince, leaving Wangenheim's corps isolated about Todtenhausen, led the whole of the rest of the army a short march to the south-west, and encamped between Fredewald and Hille. Headquarters were at Hille, under guard of the Twelfth and Twentieth Regiments of the British Foot, for the red-coats held the place of honour on the right of the line; and picquets were pushed on to Sud Hemmern, Hartum, and Hahlen, villages on the eastern side of Hille, by the border of the morass. Finally, from two to three thousand men were ordered to Lübbecke to maintain communication with the hereditary prince.

Such dispositions might well have appeared hazardous; but Ferdinand had thought them out in every detail. Wangenheim's corps, though isolated, was strongly entrenched, with several guns; while his position covered the only outlet by which the French could debouch from behind the marsh. Thereby two important objects were gained. First, the safe passage of convoys from the Lower Weser was assured; and secondly, it was made certain that, before Contades could deploy to attack Wangenheim in force, Ferdinand with the main army would have time either to fall upon his flank or simply to join his own left to Wangenheim's right. To ensure the swift execution of this latter critical movement, Ferdinand directed all generals to acquaint themselves carefully with the ground, and in particular with the outlets that led from his position to the open plain before Minden.

Contades meanwhile reasoned, as Ferdinand had hoped and intended, in a very different fashion. The Allied army was, to his mind, dispersed in every direction. Ten thousand men were with the hereditary prince at Gohfeld; at least two thousand more at Lübbecke; Ferdinand himself, with the greater portion of the army, seemed so anxious to be within supporting distance of the prince that he had left Wangenheim in the air; while even Wangenheim's corps was not

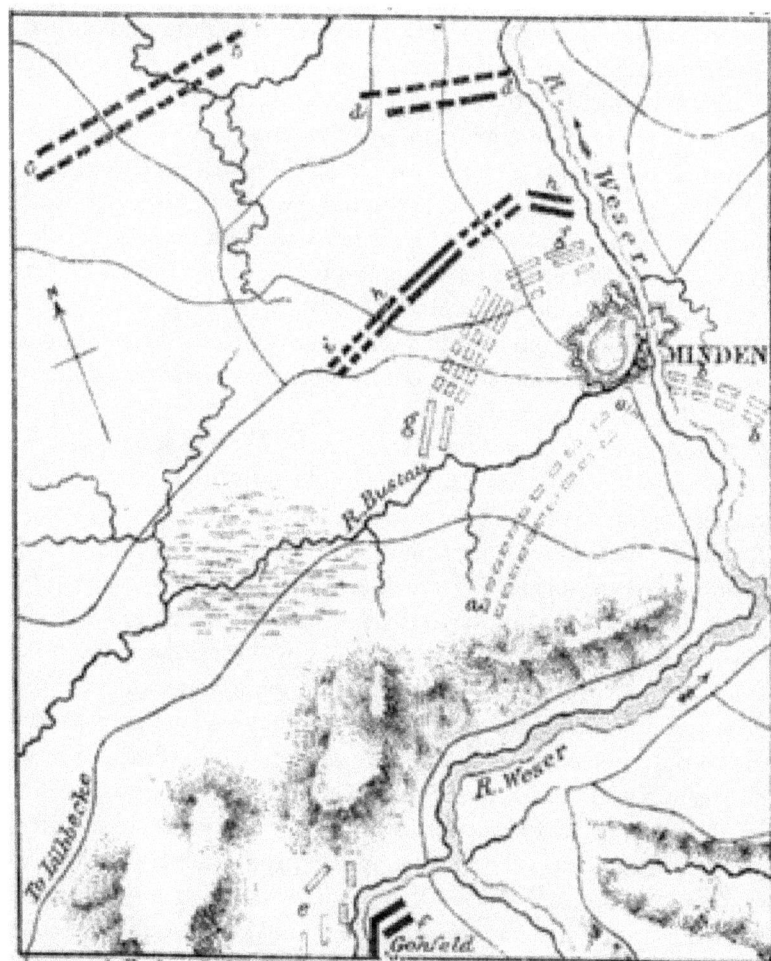

BATTLE OF MINDEN
August 1, 1759.

a a, French Army behind Minden, July 31.
b b, Broglio's detachment.
c c, The Allied Army, July 31.
d d, Wangenheim.
e, The Duc de Brissac.
f, The Hereditary Prince.
g g, French Army in battle order, August 1.
h h, Allied Army about to attack, August 1.
i, Cavalry under Sackville.

united, but had detached a few battalions across the river to keep an eye on Broglie. Still the interruption of his own communications with Cassel was troublesome; and it would be well to put an end to that and to all other difficulties by a decisive blow and a brilliant victory.

He therefore despatched the Duke of Brissac with eight thousand men to Gohfeld to hold the hereditary prince in check, threw eight bridges over the Bastau for the passage of his troops across it in as many columns, and ordered Broglie to be ready to cross the Weser with his corps to form a ninth column upon his right. The total force which he could bring into the plain of Minden was fifty-one thousand men with one hundred and sixty-two guns. Against it, if all went well, Ferdinand could oppose forty-one thousand men and one hundred and seventy guns.

A fresh gale was blowing from the south-west which drowned the stroke of the clocks of Minden, as midnight closed the last day of July and ushered in the first of August. Already the French camp was all alert in the darkness, and the columns were moving off, not without confusion, to the bridges of the Bastau. An hour later two white-coated deserters were brought in by a picquet to the Prince of Anhalt, general officer of the day in the Allied Army, with the important intelligence that the whole French Army was in motion. Ferdinand had seen signs of some stir on the previous evening, and had directed that, on the observance of the slightest movement at the advanced posts, information should be brought to him at once. Yet two o'clock came, and three o'clock, before a belated messenger arrived at headquarters from Anhalt with the news. Instantly Ferdinand called the whole of his troops to arms, and ordered them to march to their appointed positions. His orders had already been issued, and were clear and precise enough.

The advance was to be in eight columns, and the formation for battle, as usual, with infantry in the centre and cavalry on each flank. The first or right-hand column consisted of twenty-four squadrons of cavalry under Lord George Sackville, fifteen of them being British squadrons of the Blues, First and Third Dragoon Guards, Scots Greys, and Tenth Dragoons. The second was made up entirely of German artillery; and the third under Major-General von Spörcke comprised the Twelfth, Twentieth, Twenty-Third, Twenty-Fifth, Thirty-Seventh, and Fifty-First regiments of the British Line. Seven out of the eight columns were formed and marched off with great promptitude; but in Sackville's column all was confusion and delay. Some of the regiments were ready and others were not; and Sackville himself was not to be found. It was no good beginning for the British cavalry.

Having given the alarm Ferdinand hastened, with a single staff-officer accompanying him, to see for himself how matters stood. It is not difficult to conceive of his anxiety. Owing to the unpardonable neglect of Anhalt the French had gained two hours upon him; and now, when the army had been at last set in motion, the cavalry of his right wing was not moving with the rest. There was therefore every likelihood that the village of Hahlen, on which he had intended to rest his right flank, might be occupied by the French before Sackville could be there to prevent them. Instantly galloping away to Hartum he ordered the picquets stationed therein to move at once to Hahlen, and then hurried back with all speed to the latter village, only to learn the bad news that it was already in possession of the French. Meanwhile not a word had come from Wangenheim, who, for aught he knew, might be in serious difficulties. Despatching his solitary *aide-de-camp* to Todtenhausen to ascertain how matters were going on the left, he galloped on alone with his groom into the plain of Minden. The wind was blowing so furiously that not a sound even of cannon could be heard in the direction of the Weser; but before long he caught sight of the French advancing on Kuttenhausen, and of a dense cloud of smoke rising before Todtenhausen. Evidently Wangenheim was hotly engaged.

But meanwhile from windward there came the roar of a furious cannonade about Hille, where the causeway issued from the western end of the morass. This could only be a diversion, for Ferdinand had already sealed up the outlet of the causeway with five hundred men and two guns; but to make assurance still surer he now ordered two more guns and the detachment from Lübbecke to Hille, and sent information to the Hereditary Prince of what was passing. Then, galloping for a moment to the left, Ferdinand satisfied himself that his columns were advancing, and turned back in the teeth of the wind to Hahlen.

There once again the stupidity of the Prince of Anhalt had set matters wrong. He had duly brought up the picquets from Hartum before Hahlen, as directed, but had halted instead of clearing the French out of the village, and had thereby delayed the deployment of the whole of Spörcke's column. He was bidden to take the village at once, which he did without difficulty; but having done so this hopeless officer proceeded to install himself and his picquets as if to stay there forever.[3]

---

3. "*A n'en bouger plus*" are Ferdinand's own words. His exasperation against Anhalt was evidently extreme.

After the occupation of Hahlen, however, matters on the right began to adjust themselves. Ferdinand ordered Captain Foy's battery to the front of the village to cover the formation of the troops, and was soon satisfied by the admirable working of these British guns that all was safe in that quarter. Meanwhile his *aide-de-camp* returned from Todtenhausen with intelligence that Wangenheim was holding his own, though the enemy had gained ground on his right, where his flank was uncovered. Probably few commanders have passed through two worse hours than did Ferdinand at the opening of the Battle of Minden.

Fortunately for him the French had not executed their own manoeuvres without confusion and delay. It was one defect of Contades's position that he could not debouch from behind the morass by daylight, since he would have brought Ferdinand down instantly upon his flank; and the indiscipline of the French army among both officers and men was not calculated to favour orderly movement in the dark. Broglie, a capable officer, had crossed the river, taken up his appointed position on the right, and made his dispositions to fall upon Wangenheim, punctually and in good order; but he dared not attack until the rest of the army was formed, so contented himself with a simple duel of artillery. The rest of the columns shuffled here and there in helplessness and confusion; and it was not until Broglie had waited for two full hours that most of them were at last deployed in some kind of order. The French line-of-battle was convex in form, following, as it were, the contour of the walls of Minden, with the right resting on the Weser and the left on the morass.

Broglie's corps on the right was drawn up in two lines, the first of infantry, the second of cavalry, with two powerful batteries in advance. On his left stood half of the infantry of Contades's army in two lines, with thirty-four guns before them. Next to these, in the centre, were fifty-five squadrons of cavalry in two lines, with a third line of eighteen more in reserve; and next to this mass of horse stood the left wing, composed of the rest of the infantry in two lines, with thirty guns. Thus to all intent the French line-of-battle consisted of a centre of cavalry with wings of infantry; but the left wing of infantry was late in arriving at its position, and its tardiness was not without effect on the issue of the action.

Observing the excellent practice of Foy's battery before Hahlen, Ferdinand had already sent Macbean's British battery to join it and ordered Hase's Hanoverian brigade of heavy guns to the same position. Then seeing Spörcke's column of British infantry in the act of deployment, he sent orders that its advance, when the time should come, should be made with drums beating. The order was either misdelivered or misunderstood, for to his surprise the leading British brigade shook itself up and began to advance forthwith. A flight of *aides-de-camp* galloped off to stop them; and the line of scarlet halted behind a belt of fir-wood to await the formation of the rest of the army. In the first line of Spörcke's division stood, counting from right to left, the Twelfth, Thirty-Seventh, and Twenty-Third, under Brigadier Waldegrave; and in the second, which extended beyond the first on each flank, the Twentieth, Fifty-First, and Twenty-Fifth, under Brigadier Kingsley, Hardenberg's Hanoverian battalion, and two battalions of Hanoverian guards.

There then they stood for a few minutes, while the second line, which was only partially deployed, hastened to complete the evolution; when suddenly to the general amazement the drums again began to roll, and the first line stepped off once more, advancing rapidly but in perfect order, straight upon the French horse. The second line, though its formation was still incomplete, stepped off likewise in rear of its comrades, deploying as it moved, and therefore of necessity dropping somewhat in rear. And so the nine battalions, with the leading brigade far in advance, swung proudly forward into a cross-fire of more than sixty cannon, alone and unsupported from the rest of the line.

No *aide-de-camp*, gallop though he might, could stop them now; and their majestic bearing showed that they would not easily be stopped by an enemy. The British, being on the right, were the more exposed to destruction, for the French batteries on their left were too remote to maintain a really deadly fire; but what signified a cross-fire and three lines of horse to regiments that had fought at Dettingen and Fontenoy? For nearly two hundred yards of the advance the French guns tore great gaps in their ranks; but they passed through the tempest of shot unbroken and untamed, and pressed on with the same majestic steadiness against the huge motionless bank of the French horse. Then at last the wall of men and horses started into life, and eleven squadrons coming forward from the rest bore straight down upon them.

The scarlet battalions stood firm until the enemy were within ten yards of them; then pouring in one volley which strewed the ground with men and horses, they hurled the squadrons back in confused fragments upon their comrades, and continued their advance. Ferdi-

MINDEN
August 1st 1759

MILES
0 1 2

MINDEN
R. Weser

WARBURG

WARBURG
R. Diemel

MILES
0 1 2 3

VELLINGHAUSEN

WILHELMSTHAL

nand, perceiving the disorder of the French, sent an *aide-de-camp* at full speed to Lord George Sackville to bring up the British cavalry and complete the rout. Sackville disputed the meaning of the order for a time, and then advancing his squadrons for a short distance, as if to obey it, brought them once more to a halt. A second messenger came up in hot haste to ask why the cavalry of the right did not come on, but Sackville remained stationary, and the opportunity was lost.

Then shamed and indignant at their defeat the French horse rallied. Four brigades of infantry and thirty-two guns came forward from the French left to enfilade the audacious British foot; and Ferdinand, since Sackville would not move, advanced Phillips's brigade of heavy guns in order to parry, if possible, this flanking attack. Then the second line of the French horse came thundering down, eager to retrieve their defeat, upon the nine isolated battalions. For a moment the lines of scarlet seemed to waver under this triple attack; but recovering themselves they closed up their ranks and met the charging squadrons with a storm of musketry which blasted them off the field. Then turning with equal fierceness upon the French infantry they beat them also back with terrible loss.

Again an *aide-de-camp* flew from Ferdinand's side to Sackville, adjuring him to bring up the British squadrons only, if no more, to make good the success; but it was not jealousy of the foreign squadrons under his command that kept Sackville back. The messenger delivered his order; but not a squadron moved. Meanwhile Ferdinand had hurried forward fresh battalions on his right to save the British from annihilation; and now the third line of French horse, the *gendarmerie* and the *carbineers*, essayed a third attack upon the nine dauntless battalions and actually broke through the first line; but was shattered to pieces by the second and sent the way of its fellows. A fourth messenger was sent to Sackville, but with no result. Ferdinand's impatience waxed hot.

"When is that cavalry coming?" he kept exclaiming. "Has no one seen that cavalry of the right wing?" But no cavalry came.

"Good God! is there no means of getting that cavalry to advance," he ejaculated in desperation, and sent a fifth messenger to bring up Lord Granby with the squadrons of Sackville's second line only. Granby was about to execute the order, when Sackville rode up and forbade him; and then, as if still in doubt as to these repeated orders, Sackville trotted up to Ferdinand and asked what they might mean.

"My Lord," Ferdinand is said to have answered, calmly, but with such contempt as may be imagined, "the opportunity is now passed."

Nevertheless the astonishing attack of the British infantry had virtually gained the day. Ferdinand's line had gained time to form and to join with Wangenheim's; and the guns of the Allies coming up gradually in increasing force silenced the inferior artillery of the French. Ferdinand's left wing then took the offensive, and the German cavalry by a brilliant charge dispersed the whole of the infantry opposed to them. Between nine and ten o'clock the struggle was practically over. The French were completely beaten, and retreating rapidly under the guns of Minden to their pinfold behind the marsh. Had Sackville's cavalry come forward when it was bidden, it might have cut the flying French squadrons to pieces, barred the retreat of most if not all of the French left wing, and turned the victory into one of the greatest of all time. As things happened, it fell to Foy and MacBean of the British Artillery to gather the laurels of the pursuit. Hard though they had worked all day, these officers limbered up their guns and moved with astonishing rapidity along the border of the marsh, halting from time to time to pound the retreating masses of the enemy; till at last they unlimbered for good opposite the bridges of the Bastau and punished the fugitives so heavily that they would not be rallied until they had fled far beyond their camp.

Meanwhile the hereditary prince had engaged the Duke of Brissac at Gohfeld and defeated him, so that the French communications with Hervorden and Paderborn were hopelessly severed. The news of this misfortune seems to have smitten Contades almost with panic. Had he chosen to fall back by the line of his advance he could hardly have been stopped by the inferior force of the hereditary prince, and he would have found supplies and a good position at Hervorden. But his defeat had crushed all spirit out of him. Abandoning his communications with Paderborn he crossed the Weser in the night, broke down the bridge of Minden, burned his bridges of boats, and retired through a difficult and distressing country to Cassel, with an army not only beaten but demoralised.

So ended the battle of Minden, a day at once of pride and disgrace to the British. The losses of the Allies amounted to twenty-six hundred killed and wounded, of which the share of the British amounted to close on fourteen hundred men.[4]

Of the six devoted regiments who went into action four thousand four hundred and thirty-four strong, seventy-eight officers and twelve hundred and fifty-two men, or about thirty *per cent*, were killed or

---

4. 81 officers, 1311 men.

wounded; while the Hanoverian battalions with them, being on the left or sheltered flank, lost but twelve per cent. The heaviest sufferers were the Twelfth, which lost three hundred and two, and the Twentieth, which lost three hundred and twenty-two of all ranks; these regiments holding the place of honour on the right of the first and second lines. The casualties of the French were acknowledged in the official lists to amount to seven thousand, though the letters of Broglie and Contades state the numbers at from ten to eleven thousand; and the defeated army lost in addition the greater part of its baggage, seventeen standards and colours, and forty-three guns. From a military standpoint the most remarkable feature in the action was the skill with which Ferdinand contrived to entice his adversary into the field, reflecting perhaps even more credit on his judgment of men than on his knowledge of his profession.

Once drawn from behind the morass into the plain, Contades made singularly feeble and meaningless dispositions: and the formation of his line with cavalry in the centre and infantry on the flanks was, in the circumstances, simply grotesque. He seems indeed to have had no very clear idea as to what he really meant to do. It he had designed to overwhelm Wangenheim's isolated corps—and no doubt he had some vague notion of the kind—the obvious course was to launch Broglie straight at him independently, and himself to protect Broglie's flank with the main army. What he actually did was to turn Broglie's corps into the right wing of an united army, and so practically to fetter it for all decisive action. On the other hand, all preconcerted arrangements on both sides were upset by the extraordinary attack of the British infantry, a feat of gallantry and endurance that stands, so far as I know, absolutely without a parallel.

"I never thought," said Contades bitterly, to see a single line of infantry break through three lines of cavalry ranked in order of battle, and tumble them to ruin."

Westphalen, the chief of Ferdinand's staff, wrote grimly:

"Never, were so many boots and saddles seen on a battlefield as opposite to the English and the Hanoverian Guards."

Next to this attack the feature that seems to have attracted most attention among both contemporary and modern critics, was the remarkable efficiency of the British artillery. The handling of the artillery generally at Minden, which was entrusted to the Count of Lippe-Bückeburg, was very greatly admired: but Westphalen, who passed lightly over the deeds of the infantry, went out of his way to write that, though every battery had done well, the English batteries had done wonders. And indeed some British guns which were attached to Wangenheim's corps on the left earned not less praise than those of Foy and MacBean on the right. The palm of the cavalry fell to the Germans, and in particular to a few squadrons of Prussian dragoons lent by Frederick the Great, which earned it brilliantly. It would have fallen to the British but for Sackville.

The part played by this deplorable man did not end with the battle. Ferdinand in general orders made scathing allusion to his conduct without mentioning his name; and Sackville was presently superseded and sent home. There he was tried by court-martial and pronounced unfit to serve the king in any military capacity whatever—a hard sentence but probably no more than just. Sackville was admitted to be an extremely able man; and as he had passed through Fontenoy and been wounded in that action, it is not easy to call him a coward. But the courage of some men is not the same on every day; and the evidence produced at the court-martial shows, I think, too plainly that on the day of Minden Sackville's courage failed him.[5] The king published the sentence of his dismissal from the army in a special order, with very severe but not undeserved comment; and Lord George Sackville henceforth disappears from British battlefields.

On the day following the battle, (August 2nd), the hereditary prince crossed the Weser in pursuit of the French, and overtaking their rear-guard at Einbeck captured many prisoners and much spoil, but failed to arrest the retreat of the main body. Contades, therefore, succeeded in bringing his troops back to Cassel, half starved, worn out by hard marching, and utterly demoralised by indiscipline and pillage. D'Armentières, on hearing of his chiefs defeat, raised the siege of Lippstadt and marched eastward to meet him. Ferdinand meanwhile, having received the surrender of Minden, (Aug. 5th), advanced by Bielefeld and Paderborn south-eastward upon Corbach, so as to turn Contades's left flank. On the 18th Contades, seeing his communications endangered, evacuated Cassel and retired by forced marches to Marburg, where he took up a strong position.

Cassel capitulated to the Allies on the following day; and Ferdinand, while still pursuing his march southward, detached seven thousand men, (Aug. 24th), to recapture Münster. Marshal d'Estrées then arrived (Aug. 25th), to supersede Contades; but little came of this change of command. Renewed menace from the westward upon the

5. Mauvillon has a curious and striking passage on the subject.

French communications forced him to withdraw from the line of the Ohm and Lahn, and to fall back to Giessen. Ferdinand at once laid siege to Marburg, which fell within a week, and finally on the 19th of September he encamped at Kroffdorf, a little to northwest of Giessen, over against the French camp.

Meanwhile the siege of Münster had gone ill for the Allies, and had been turned into a blockade. Ferdinand, after sending additional troops thither, found himself too weak to attempt further operations until the fall of the town, (Nov. 21st); and during this interval Broglie, who had been appointed to the supreme command, had received a reinforcement of ten thousand Würtembergers. Thus strengthened he tried incessantly with a detached corps of twenty thousand men to interrupt Ferdinand's communications with Cassel, but in vain; and finally the hereditary prince attacked this corps at Fulda, defeated it signally, and then turning upon Broglie's right flank forced him to retire to Friedberg. Ferdinand then blockaded Giessen; but at this point further operations were stayed. Ever since his disastrous defeat by the Russians at Kunersdorf in August, Frederick the Great had pressed Ferdinand for reinforcements; and the detachment of twelve thousand troops to the king not only rendered the prince powerless for further aggression, but obliged him also to raise the blockade of Giessen.

In January 1760 both armies retired into winter-quarters. The French occupied much the same ground as at the beginning of the campaign; and the Allies likewise were distributed into two divisions, the army of Westphalia extending from Münster through Paderborn to the Weser, the army of Hesse from Marburg eastward to the Werra. Thus ended the campaign of 1759, leaving both parties in occupation of the same territory as at its beginning; but it had branded the French with the discredit of a great defeat, and had heightened in the Allies their contempt for their enemy and their confidence in their chief.

CHAPTER 8

Emsdorff & Warburg

Never in the whole course of her history had come to England such a year of triumph as 1759. Opening with the capture of Goree in January, its later months had brought one unbroken tale of success, of Madras saved and Masulipatam taken in India, of Quebec captured in Canada, of Minden won in Germany, of one French fleet worsted by Boscawen off the Portuguese coast, of another defeated by Hawke in the romantic action of Quiberon Bay. Such was the story with which King George the Second met his Parliament for the last time in his life; and Pitt did not fail to turn it to good account. A monument was voted to Wolfe in Westminster Abbey; thanks were given to Hawke, Saunders and Holmes of the Navy, and to Monckton, Murray and Townsend of the Army; and the military estimates were passed with little difficulty. It was ordered that Ferdinand's army should be augmented from Great Britain, Brunswick, and Hesse alike. The full number of national troops voted for the British Establishment exceeded one hundred thousand men; the embodied militia augmented this total by twenty thousand, and the German troops in the pay of England by fifty-five thousand more; while another twelve thousand men at home and abroad, which were borne on the Irish Establishment, raised it to close on one hundred and ninety thousand men.

Before the campaign of 1760 was opened, the infantry of the British Line had increased to ninety-six regiments; England contributing one new corps, Wales one, Scotland five, and Ireland four, all of which were disbanded at the close of the war.[1] To these there were added

1. These regiments with their dates of formation are as follows: 85th, Crawfurd's Volunteers, 21st July 1759; 86th, Worge's (for Goree), 24th August 1759; 87th, Keith's Highlanders, 25th August 1759; 88th, Campbell's Highland Volunteers, 1st January 1760; 89th, Morris's Highlanders, 13th October 1759; 90th, (continued next page),

later in the year six new regiments of light dragoons. The first was formed in August under Colonel John Burgoyne, which took rank as the Sixteenth Dragoons, and is now known to us as the Sixteenth Lancers; the second, created in October by Lord Aberdour, soon perished and left no mark behind it; and the third was raised under rather remarkable conditions by Colonel John Hale in November. Colonel Hale, originally of the Blues and later of the Forty-Third Foot, was the officer who brought back the despatches reporting the victory of Quebec. Finding on his arrival in England in October that there was still some alarm of a French invasion, he volunteered to form a regiment of the footmen and chairmen of London and to lead them against the best household troops of France; an offer which so delighted Pitt that he reported it to the House of Commons. Finally, he engaged himself to raise a strong regiment of light dragoons without levy- money for men or horses, promising that any men or horses objected to on review by the inspecting officer should be replaced without expense to the country, and that the whole corps should be completed within two months.

The offer was accepted, and the regiment was raised at the sole expense of the officers within the space, as it is said, of seventeen days. The number was not inappropriate; for though first known, during the few years while Aberdour's lasted, as the Eighteenth, this regiment, still conspicuous by the white facings and the badge of skull and crossbones which Hale selected for it, remains with us as the Seventeenth Lancers. The three remaining corps, which raised the number of regiments of dragoons to twenty-one, were too short-lived to merit more than mere mention.[2]

The menace of French invasion was rather ludicrously realised in February by a descent of the French privateer, Thurot, with five ships upon Carrickfergus. Landing about a thousand troops, he received the surrender of the town after a skirmish with the garrison, plundered it, contrary to the terms of the capitulation, and re-embarked. His squadron, however, was almost immediately caught by three British

Morgan's (Irish), 7th December 1759; 91st, Blayney's (Irish), 12th January 1760; 92nd, Gore's (Irish), 17th January 1760; 93rd, Bagshawe's (Irish), 17th January 1760; 94th, Vaughan's (Welsh), 12th January 1760; Campbell's Argyleshire Fencibles, 21st July 1759; Sutherland's Highlanders, 11th August 1757. These numbers, of course, disappeared at the close of the war, when the regiments were disbanded. The two last named were never numbered.

2. They were Drogheda's (19th Light Dragoons), November 1759; Caldwell's (20th Light Dragoons), 12th January 1760; Granby's (21st Royal Foresters), 5th April 1760.

men-of-war, when after a short action Thurot was killed and every one of his ships captured. This tragic termination to Thurot's escapade relieved the general tension, and restored the country's confidence.

So foolish a raid was not likely to produce any change in Pitt's preparations for the reinforcement of Ferdinand, who needed to be specially strengthened after the disasters that had befallen King Frederick at Kunersdorf and at Maxen. In January it was decided to send three more regiments of British cavalry to Germany; and a few weeks later the number was increased to five. In May a further reinforcement of six battalions and two regiments of Highlanders was promised, and in June two additional regiments of cavalry; making up a total of close on ten thousand men.[3] The troops were shipped to the Weser instead of, as heretofore, to Emden, and seem to have been despatched with commendable promptitude; for the six regiments of foot, though only warned for service on the 1st of May, were actually reviewed by Ferdinand in his camp at Fritzlar on the 17th of June, and were declared by him to be in a most satisfactory condition.

The campaign of 1759 having been prolonged so far into the winter, Ferdinand gave his army rest until late in May. At length on the 20th he called the infantry of the army of Hesse from its cantonments, and posted the main body under his own command at Fritzlar, with one corps advanced to Hersfeld on the Fulda to protect his left, and a second under General Imhoff at Kirchhain, on the Ohm. It was his intention that, in case of the enemy's advance, Imhoff should call in the detachment from Hersfeld to Homberg, a little to the south of Kirchhain on a bend of the Ohm, where there was a position, before long to be better known to us, in which he could bar the way to a far superior force. Simultaneously the army of Westphalia moved to its line of the previous year, from Coesfeld eastward to Hamm.

In these positions the Allies remained for nearly a month before the French made the least sign of movement; when at last the army of the Lower Rhine under the Count of St. Germain assembled at Düsseldorf, (June 20th), and crossing the Rhine advanced to Dortmund. From this centre it was open to St. Germain to advance either northward against Münster or eastward against Lippstadt; but it was tolerably evident that his real design was to join the army of the Main, and to operate against the right flank of the Allied army of Hesse, (June 22nd).

---

3. The regiments despatched were the 2nd, 6th and 7th Dragoon Guards; 1st, 7th, 11th Dragoons, and 15th Light Dragoons; the 5th, 8th, 11th, 24th, 33rd, 50th Foot. The 15th and 7th were not sent until June.

At about the same time Broglie concentrated the army of the Main a little to the east of Giessen, and began his advance northward. The Hereditary Prince at once fell back from Hersfeld with his detachment towards the Ohm, while Ferdinand moved southward as far as Ziegenhain to join Imhoff, with every intention of making Broglie fight him before he advanced another mile. To his infinite disgust, however, he learned that Imhoff had abandoned the position entrusted to him, and had ordered the whole of the advanced corps back to Kirchhain. Thus the most effective barrier in Hesse was opened to the French, (June 24th); Ferdinand perforce halted; and Broglie pushed on without delay to Homberg, whence turning eastward he encamped in the face of Ferdinand's army at Neustadt. In this situation both armies remained for a whole fortnight inactive, though not two hours' march apart, neither daring to attack the other, and each waiting for the other to make the next movement.

Broglie brought the deadlock to an end. Sending orders to St. Germain to march from Dortmund on the 4th of July, and to meet him at Corbach, he marched on the night of the 7th north-westward upon Frankenberg. Ferdinand on learning of his movements next day marched also northward with all speed, pushing forward a strong advanced corps under the hereditary prince by way of Sachsenhausen upon Corbach, to bar the outlet of the defile through which Broglie's army must pass into the plain, and so to hinder his junction with St. Germain. The French, however, had gained too long a start.

St. Germain, though he distressed his troops terribly by the speed of his march, succeeded in passing through the defile from the north; and Broglie, hastening up from the south, found his troops forming in order of battle, (July 10th), just as the hereditary prince debouched into the plain from Sachsenhausen. As not more than ten thousand of the French were yet deployed, the prince attacked; but was soon driven back by superior numbers as the rest of the French came up, and finally retired with the loss of five hundred men and fifteen guns, seven of which last were British. It fell to the British infantry with the prince, the Fifth, Twenty-Fourth, Fiftieth, and Fifty-First regiments, to cover the retreat; but so hard were they pressed that the prince only extricated them by putting himself at the head of two squadrons of the First and Third Dragoon Guards, and leading them to a desperate charge. Fortunately the squadrons responded superbly,[4] and so the rear-guard

---

4. The First Dragoon Guards went into this charge with ninety men and returned with twenty-four.

was saved; but the prince had received an unpleasant reverse, and the French had secured their first object with signal success.

The Allied army of Westphalia, under General von Spörcke, arrived on the scene in obedience to orders two days after the action, (July 12th), and was posted at Volksmarsen on the Diemel to protect Ferdinand's right; and then once more the two hosts remained motionless and face to face, the French at Corbach, the Allies at Sachsenhausen. Ferdinand's total force was sixty-six thousand men only, while that of the French numbered one hundred and thirty thousand; [5] yet such was the difference in the quality of the two armies that Broglie dared not act except with extreme caution. His principal object was to envelope Ferdinand's right and cut him off from Westphalia at the line of the Diemel; and Ferdinand accordingly resolved to distract Broglie's attention to the opposite flank.

Having intelligence that a party of the enemy under General Glaubitz, consisting of six battalions, a regiment of Hussars, and a number of light troops, was on its way to Ziegenhain from Marburg, evidently with the object of disturbing his communications, Ferdinand, on the night of the 14th, detached the hereditary prince to take command of six battalions which were lying at Fritzlar, and to attack it. Accordingly on the following morning the prince marched rapidly southward, being joined on the way by a regiment of German hussars, and by the Fifteenth Light Dragoons, which had just arrived from England. On reaching the vicinity of Ziegenhain, he found that Glaubitz was encamped farther to the west, near the village of Emsdorff. His troops being exhausted by a long march, the prince halted for the night at Treysa, and continuing his advance early on the morrow, picked up two more bodies of irregulars, horse and foot, which were on their way to him, and pushed on with his mounted troops only, to reconnoitre the enemy's position.

He found the French posted at the mouth of a gorge in the mountains, fronting to north-east, astride of the two roads that lead from Kirchhain to Fritzlar and to Ziegenhain. Their right lay in rear of the village of Emsdorff, and their left in front of the village of Emsdorff, resting on a forest some three miles long. The prince and General Lückner, who was with him, entered the forest, but found neither picquets nor sentries; they pushed forward through the corn-fields to within half a mile of the camp, but saw neither vedettes, nor patrols, nor so much as a main-guard; nay, Emsdorff itself, though within less

---

5. Westphalen IV. 313, 353. The numbers are from official sources.

than a mile of the camp, was not occupied. They stole back well content with what they had seen.

Waiting till eleven o'clock for his infantry to join him, the prince posted one battalion, Lückner's regiment of hussars and the Fifteenth Light Dragoons, in a hollow a mile before Emsdorff; then taking the five remaining battalions, together with the irregular troops and four guns, he fetched a compass through the forest and came in full upon the enemy's left flank. The French were completely surprised. Two battalions had barely time to form towards the forest before the prince's infantry came upon them, poured in a volley which laid three hundred men low, and drove back the rest upon Glaubitz's remaining infantry, which was falling in hurriedly in rear of the camp. Simultaneously Lückner, at the sound of the firing, came galloping up on the French right with his cavalry; whereupon the entire French force abandoned its camp and retired through the woods in their rear towards Langenstein. Here they rallied; but Lückner's single battalion hurried on beyond them to bar their way over the Ohm to westward, while the Fifteenth, pressing on along their flank, stationed itself across the road to Amöneberg, and charging full upon them headed them back from that side.

With some difficulty the French repelled the attack, and turning about to south-eastward made for a wood not far away, hoping to pass through it and so to escape to the south. But on arriving at the southern edge of the wood they found every outlet blocked by the prince's mounted irregulars. Perforce they turned back through the wood again and emerged on to the open ground on its western side, trusting that some marshy ground, which lay in the way of the prince's cavalry, would secure them from further pursuit. But they had not marched over the plain for more than a mile before the hussars and light dragoons were upon them again, and the Fifteenth for the second time crashed single-handed into the midst of them, cutting them down by scores and capturing one battalion complete.

With great difficulty the remnant of the French beat back their pursuers and continued the retreat: half of them had been killed or captured, or had dropped down unable to march farther, but the rest struggled gallantly on. Reaching an open wood they again halted and formed for action. The prince, still close at their heels with his cavalry, thereupon surrounded them and summoned them to surrender; and the French commander, despairing of further resistance in the exhausted state of his troops, was obliged to yield.

So ended the action which is still commemorated on the appointments of the Fifteenth Hussars by the name of Emsdorff. The French camp had been surprised at noon; and the last fragment of their force capitulated at six o'clock in the evening, having striven manfully but in vain to shake off the implacable enemy that had hunted them for nearly twenty miles. The loss of the French in killed and wounded is unknown, though it must have been considerable, but the prisoners taken numbered twenty-six hundred, while nine colours and five guns were also captured. The total loss of the prince's troops did not exceed one hundred and eight-six men and one hundred and eighty-one horses, of which one hundred and twenty-five men and one hundred and sixty-eight horses belonged to the Fifteenth.

It was the Fifteenth, in fact, that did all the fighting. The other regiments engaged did not lose twenty men apiece. The infantry could not keep pace with the pursuit after they reached Langenstein, and the two other corps of cavalry, though they did excellent work in heading back the enemy, never came to close quarters. Lückner's hussars did not lose a man nor a horse, and of the mounted irregulars but twenty-three men and horses were killed or wounded. It was the Fifteenth alone, a young regiment that had never been under fire, which thrice charged five times its numbers of French infantry and rode through them; and the success of the action was ascribed to them and to them only. Their gallantry indeed was the amazement of the whole army.[6] The tradition of charging home, as shall be seen in due time both in Flanders and in Spain, remained with the regiment, and doubtless remains with it to this day.

This brilliant exploit was some compensation to the Allies for past mishaps; but a week later Broglie sought to turn the scale by more serious operations. On the 23rd he divided his army into three corps, of which he sent one round Ferdinand's left flank under Prince Xavier of Saxony to threaten Cassel, and a second to force back Spörcke on his right from Volksmarsen, while the main body under his own command advanced to Sachsenhausen. Perforce Ferdinand retreated north-westward to Kalle, his rear-guard being incessantly and severely engaged throughout the movement, (July 25th-27th); whereupon Broglie, seeing the way to be clear, detached a corps under the Chevalier de Muy, who had recently arrived to relieve the Count of St. Germain, across the Diemel to Warburg, in order to cut off the Allies from Westphalia. The marshal himself meanwhile moved up parallel

6. Mauvillon

119

to Ferdinand on the eastern side towards Kalle, and Prince Xavier pressed still closer upon Cassel.

It being evident to Ferdinand that either Cassel or Westphalia must be abandoned, he detached a force under General Kielmansegge to strengthen the garrison of Cassel and resolved to attack de Muy. Accordingly, on the afternoon of the 29th Spörcke's corps crossed the Diemel to Liebenau, followed on the same evening by that of the hereditary prince; and on the 30th their combined force, not exceeding in all fourteen thousand men, encamped between Liebenau and Corbeke with its left on the Diemel, facing west. At dawn of the same morning Broglie's army debouched from several quarters simultaneously against the Allied camp at Kalle, but drew off after some hours of cannonade; and Ferdinand, satisfied through other signs that this demonstration was intended only to cover the movement of the French towards Cassel, resolved to pass the Diemel without delay and to deliver his stroke against de Muy.

Spörcke and the hereditary prince had meanwhile reconnoitred de Muy's position and had recommended that their own corps should turn its left flank, while Ferdinand with the main army advanced against its front. De Muy, with about twenty thousand men, occupied a high ridge across a bend of the Diemel, facing north-east, with his right resting on Warburg and his left near the village of Ochsendorf. To his left rear rose a circular hill crowned by a tower, and on his left front lay a village named Poppenheim. It was arranged that the corps of Spörcke and the hereditary prince should advance westward in two columns from Corbeke and form up in three lines between the tower and Poppenheim, so as to fall on de Muy's left flank and rear, while Ferdinand crossing the Diemel at Liebenau should attack his centre and right. As the camp between Liebenau and Corbeke lay about ten miles from de Muy's, and as Ferdinand's camp lay some fifteen miles to the south of the Diemel from Liebenau, the operation called for extreme nicety in the execution.

At nine o'clock on the evening of the 30th Ferdinand's army marched from Kalle, and at six o'clock on the following morning the heads of his columns passed the Diemel and debouched on the heights of Corbeke. They arrived, however, at later than the appointed hour. The passage of the Diemel had caused much delay; and not all the haste of officers nor the eagerness of men could bring the army forward the quicker. At seven o'clock Spörcke and the hereditary prince, after much anxious waiting, decided to march from Corbeke before more time should be lost. The northern column, which included the right wing of all three arms, moved by Gross Eider and Ochsendorf upon the tower; the southern, composed of the left wing, by Klein Eider and Poppenheim. Both columns were led by British troops— the northern by the Royal Dragoons, whose place was on the extreme right of the first line, while the British grenadiers, massed in two battalions under Colonels Maxwell and Daulhatt,[7] marched at the head of the infantry. The southern was headed by the Seventh Dragoons, with Keith's and Campbell's Highlanders[8] following them to cover the grenadiers in second line.

At half-past one the hereditary prince, having posted his artillery on the outskirts of Ochsendorf of Poppenheim, opened fire as the signal for attack; and at the same time the British grenadiers began to file through Ochsendorf. Certain French battalions, which de Muy had thrown back *en potence* to protect his left flank, thereupon retired without firing, until it was perceived that the Allies were making for the steep hill in rear of the French position. Then one battalion of Regiment Bourbonnois deliberately faced about and marched off to occupy the hill. To permit such a thing would have been to derange the whole of the plans of the Allies, so it was necessary to prevent it at any cost. Colonel Beckwith with ten grenadiers ran forward, keeping out of sight of the French, to reach the hill before them; the prince himself with thirty more hurried after him; and with this handful of men, all panting and breathless, they crowned the crest of the height. Bourbonnois arriving on the scene a little later found itself greeted by a sharp fire, and, being unable to see the numbers opposed to it, halted for ten minutes to allow its second battalion to come up.

The delay gave time for Daulhatt's entire battalion of grenadiers to join Beckwith's little party; and then the two battalions of Bourbonnois attacked in earnest, and the combat between French and British, at odds of two against one, became most fierce and stubborn. The disparity of numbers however, was too great; and Daulhatt's men after a gallant struggle were beginning to give way, when Maxwell's battalion came up in the nick of time to support them. This reinforcement redressed the balance of the fight; Daulhatt's men speedily rallied, and the contest for the hill was renewed.

The French, however, prepared to send fresh battalions in sup-

---

7. Daulhatt's is set down as British in the official lists; but other evidence leads me to think that it included Hanoverian grenadiers also.
8. These two regiments then ranked as the 87th and 88th.

port of Bourbonnois, and the situation of the British became critical; for a battery of artillery, which was on its way to the hill to support them, got into difficulties in a defile near Ochsendorf and blocked the advance of the rest of the northern column. Fortunately it was extricated, though none too soon, and being brought up to the hill was speedily in action; while the head of the southern column likewise coming up took the French reinforcements in flank and drove them back in disorder. The Royals and Seventh Dragoons were then let loose upon the broken French battalions, completing their discomfiture and taking many prisoners.

So far the turning movement had succeeded; but its success was not yet assured, for only a portion of the southern column was yet formed for action, and the troops on the field were becoming exhausted. De Muy might yet have hoped to turn the scale in his left, when his attention was suddenly called to the advance of troops upon his front. After desperate but fruitless efforts it had been found that the infantry of Ferdinand's army could not hope to arrive in time to take part in the action. The British battalions, urged by General Waldegrave, struggled manfully to get forward, but the day was hot, and the ground was difficult and in many places marshy: the men would not fall out, but they dropped down insensible from fatigue in spite of themselves.

Ferdinand therefore ordered Lord Granby, who had succeeded to Sackville, to advance with the twenty-two squadrons of British cavalry and the British artillery alone. Away therefore they started at the trot, the guns accompanying them at a speed which amazed all beholders.[9] Two hours of trotting brought them at last within sight of the enemy; and Granby at once turned them upon the cavalry of de Muy's right wing. The pace was checked for a brief moment as the squadrons formed in two lines for the attack. In the first line from right to left were the First, Third, and Second Dragoon Guards, in one brigade, the Blues, Seventh, and Sixth Dragoon Guards in another; in the second line were the Greys, Tenth, Sixth, and Eleventh Dragoons. Then the advance was resumed, Granby riding at the head of the Blues, his own regiment, and well in front of all. His hat flew from his head, revealing a bald head which shone conspicuous in the sun, as the trot grew into gallop and the lines came thundering on.

The French squadrons wavered for a moment, and then, with the exception of three only, turned and fled without awaiting the shock. The scarlet ranks promptly wheeled round upon the flank and rear of

9. Tempelhof.

122

the French infantry; whereupon the three French squadrons that had stood firm plunged gallantly down on the flank of the King's Dragoon Guards, and overthrew them. But the Blues quickly came up to liberate their comrades; and the devoted little band of Frenchmen was cut to pieces. The French infantry, finding itself now attacked on both flanks, broke and fled; and the whole of de Muy's men, horse and foot, rushed down to the Diemel, and, without even looking for the bridges, threw down their arms and splashed frantically through the fords. A party of French irregulars in Warburg tried likewise to escape, but was caught by the cavalry and well-nigh annihilated. Finally, the British batteries came down to the river at a gallop, unlimbered on the bank, and played on the fugitives so destructively as wholly to prevent them from reforming. Granby presently crossed the river in pursuit with ten squadrons; and the fragments of de Muy's corps retired in disorder to Volksmarsen. Thus brilliantly ended the action of Warburg.

The loss of the French was set down at from six to eight thousand men, killed, wounded, and taken, while twelve guns remained as trophies in the hands of the victors. The Allies lost just over twelve hundred men, of whom no less than two hundred and forty belonged to Maxwell's grenadiers; Daulhatt's battalion also suffering very severely. The losses of the cavalry were trifling. Altogether the action was a brilliant little affair, well designed and, despite the tardiness of Ferdinand's arrival, well executed. For the British it redeemed the character of the cavalry which had been so shamefully sacrificed by Sackville at Minden; since it was evidently the recollection of that disgrace which spurred Granby on to so rapid an advance and so headlong an attack. For Ferdinand the victory effectually opened the way into Westphalia.

Meanwhile it had been found impossible to defend Cassel against Broglie's overwhelming numbers; and the town was accordingly abandoned. It was no fault of Ferdinand's that Hesse was thus laid at the mercy of the French; indeed, with an army weaker in numbers by one-half than his enemy's, he had done well to save Westphalia. He now took up a position along the Diemel from Trendelburg to Stadtbergen, so as to seal up every passage over the river, while Broglie posted his main army over against him on the opposite bank. The marshal's superiority in numbers, however, enabled him, while holding the Allies in check with the bulk of his army, to detach independent corps for minor operations, though he took even such enterprises in hand with redoubled caution after the lessons of Emsdorff and Warburg.

His first essay was the reduction of Ziegenhain, which surrendered

WARBURG,
31st July 1760.

English Miles

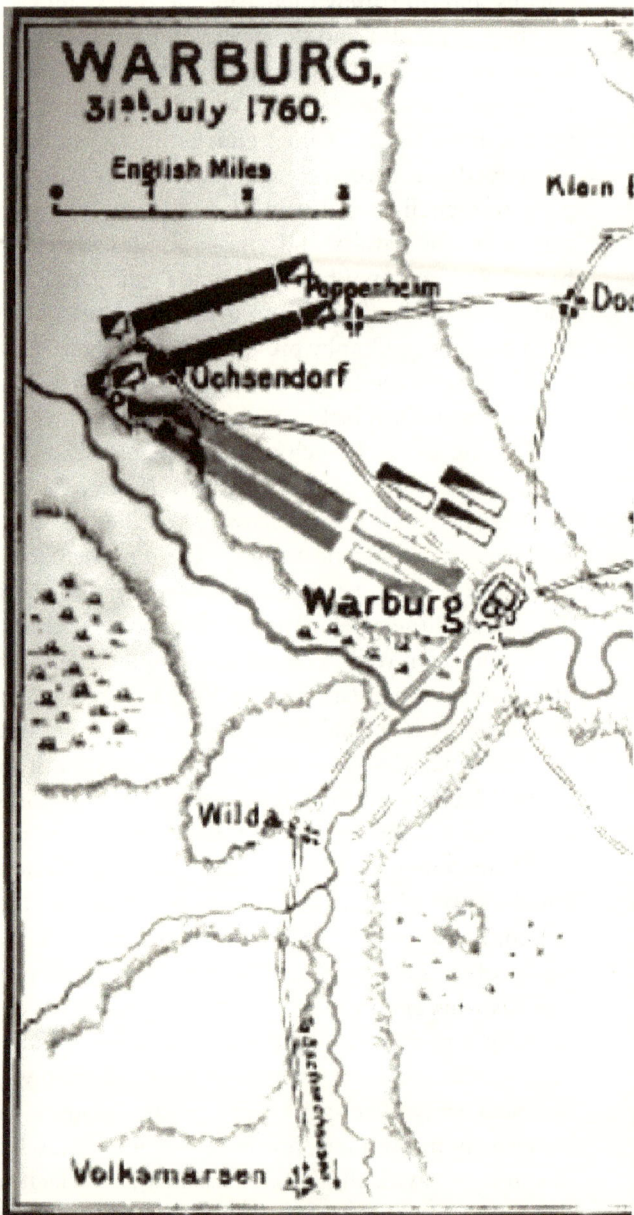

Kleın
Poppenheim
Dos
Ochsendorf
Warburg
Wilda
Volkmarsen

Borgentreich

Gross Eider

Eider

ssel

Corbeke

Desenberg

Liebenau

Diemel

k

to miles to Cassel

after a siege of ten days, (Aug. 10th); and. concurrently he moved a corps under Prince Xavier eastward against Münden, which occupied Göttingen and pushed detachments forward as far north as Nordheim and Einbeck. This latter movement carried the war unpleasantly far into Hanoverian territory; but Ferdinand none the less remained immovable on the Diemel. Broglie thereupon broke up his camp on that river and shifted his position eastward to Immenhausen, to support the operations of Prince Xavier.

This placed Ferdinand in an awkward dilemma. He had sent a few troops to Beverungen on the Weser to check Xavier's advanced parties; but this detachment, though it had done its work well, was not strong enough to make head against an invasion in real force. Moreover Einbeck was disagreeably near to the border of his brother's dominions of Brunswick, which he would fain have saved from invasion if he could. Yet he could not move to the east bank of the Weser without uncovering Lippstadt, the one fortress which enabled him to prevent the perfect concert of the French armies of the Rhine and Main. In fact the situation was one of extreme trial and embarrassment.

Ferdinand, whose light troops and irregulars were never idle while they could make mischief, first tried the effect of a raid with a flying column upon Broglie's communications with Frankfort; but this enterprise, though it alarmed the French and somewhat threw back their preparations, only partially achieved its object. On the other hand, it was always open to Ferdinand to stay where he was till want of forage should compel Broglie to retire; but this, though an infallible method, was slow, and would mean that the country would be converted into a desert, through which it would be impossible to follow the French during their retreat. He therefore resolved to make a diversion by carrying the war suddenly to the Rhine. Broglie, in his anxiety to invade Hanover and Brunswick, had denuded Wesel of the greater part of its garrison. If Ferdinand could snatch Wesel, the base of the Army of the Rhine, from him, the diversion would be a telling stroke indeed.

All through the first days of September Ferdinand's preparations for this undertaking went steadily and silently forward; and on the 22nd a powerful train of siege-artillery, under the Count of Lippe-Bückeburg, marched away for Wesel, followed three days later by the hereditary prince with about ten thousand Hanoverians and Hessians. The count was to conduct the siege and the prince to cover it. Broglie, on learning of their departure, at once detached a strong corps under the Marquis of Castries to follow them; to which Ferdinand retorted by sending to the prince one Hanoverian and ten British battalions, together with a Hessian regiment and three British regiments of cavalry.[10]

Meanwhile the prince's advanced parties had crossed the Rhine below Wesel on the 29th of September, and had surprised two or three small garrisons. The *commandant* of Wesel thereupon broke down the bridge which connected it with the western bank of the Rhine; and none too soon, for on the 30th the prince came up and invested the fortress. The siege, however, progressed but slowly owing to rain and stormy weather; and meanwhile Castries was advancing by forced marches, despite the dreadful state of the roads, along a route full fifty miles south of the prince's, to the Rhine. On the 12th of October he crossed the river at Cologne and pushed on without delay to Rheinberg, where he was joined by reinforcements from Brabant. Considering the unspeakable difficulties of foul weather and almost impassable roads, this march of Castries stands out as a very fine feat of resolution and endurance.

The advance of French troops from the side of Brabant was a complication which neither Ferdinand nor the hereditary prince had foreseen. In fact it almost deprived the advance to Wesel of the character of a diversion. Castries had in Rheinberg thirty battalions and thirty-eight squadrons besides irregular troops, and was expecting further reinforcements; whereas the prince, weakened by the absence of men in the trenches before Wesel, could muster but twenty-one battalions and twenty-two squadrons to meet him. It was open to the prince either to fight against superior numbers or to retreat; and he elected to fight. Castries had taken up a position behind the Eugenian Canal, facing north-west, with his right resting on Rheinberg, and with the abbey of Kloster Kampen, on the northern side of the canal, before his left front.

Immediately before his left, but on his own side of the canal, stood the village of Kampenbröck, consisting of several scattered houses with gardens, ditches, and hedges. In front and to the left, or western, side of Kampenbröck was a morass covered by a straggling wood of sparse and stunted trees, through which were cut paths to a bridge that connected the village with the abbey on the other side of the canal. Across this bridge lay the prince's only way to penetrate into the French camp; and Castries had been careful to guard the passage

---

10. The 11th, 20th, 23rd, 25th, 33rd, 51st Foot; two battalions of grenadiers, two more of Highlanders; the 1st, 6th, and 10th Dragoons.

by posting no less than two thousand irregular troops in and about the abbey. The only possible chance for the prince lay in an attack by surprise.

Waiting until the 15th to collect his troops, the prince marched from before Wesel in dead silence at one hour before midnight. The force was disposed in five divisions. The Fifteenth Light Dragoons, Royal and Inniskilling Dragoons, and Prussian hussars formed the advanced guard; then came the support, of two battalions of Highlanders and as many of British grenadiers; then the main body of the Twentieth and Twenty-Fifth British Foot, with eight Hanoverian battalions, all under command of General Waldegrave; then the reserve, of the Eleventh, Twenty-Third, Thirty-Third and Fifty-First British Foot, with three German battalions, under General Howard; then a rearguard of the Tenth British Dragoons and ten German squadrons.

At three o'clock on the morning of the 16th the advanced parties of the Allies come upon the outposts of the French irregulars, a mile and a half beyond Kloster Kampen. Despite the strict orders of the prince one or two shots were fired, but fortunately without alarming the enemy; and the Allies pursued their march unmolested to the bridge, thus cutting off the irregulars in the abbey from the French main body. These isolated troops were then attacked and utterly dispersed; and while the musketry was still crackling loud round the abbey's walls the prince stealing silently on with the British grenadiers penetrated into the wood and into the village of Kampenbröck, so quietly and yet so swiftly that he was in possession before the enemy were aware of his presence. The French in camp had, however, been alarmed by the firing, and some of the principal officers had turned the men out and gone forward to the wood to reconnoitre.

One of these, the Chevalier d'Assas, on his way to visit the picquets of his regiment, suddenly found himself among the British grenadiers, but distinguishing no one but the prince in the darkness advanced towards him with the words, "Sir, you are my prisoner."

"On the contrary," answered the prince, "you are mine, for these are my grenadiers"; and as he spoke the men closed round d'Assas with bayonets fixed.

"Auvergne, Auvergne, the enemy is on us," [11] shouted d'Assas to his regiment without a moment's hesitation at the top of his voice; and before the words were out of his mouth a dozen bayonets pierced through his body and laid him dead on the ground.

---

11. *À moi, Auvergne, voilà les ennemis.*

Death of Chevalier d'Assas at Kloster Kampen

None the less the devotion of the gallant man sufficed to save the French Army. Regiment Auvergne came down at once to d'Assas' call; Castries hastily brought down two more battalions to support it; and three more battalions arrived directly after to protect their flank. The supports of the Allies came up in their turn; and the fight swayed furiously backward and forward until daylight, when the French brought up additional battalions from their right. The reserves of the Allies were promptly and frequently summoned, but through some mistake were not to be found. Still the little force of British and Hanoverians fought desperately on, until the prince himself fell wounded from his horse; and then, their ammunition being exhausted, they yielded to superior numbers in front and flank and suddenly gave way.

The French broke their ranks with loud cries of exultation for the pursuit, when the Fifteenth Light Dragoons swooped down upon them, charging home as their custom is, broke up two battalions completely, and drove the rest flying back in confusion upon their comrades. The French cavalry now came forward in overwhelming numbers and handled the British squadrons very roughly; but the charge of the Fifteenth had given the infantry time to rally, and to make their retreat in good order. The reserve appeared at Kloster Kampen in time to cover the retiring troops, and by noon the fight of Kloster Kampen was over.

The loss of the Allies amounted to nearly twelve hundred killed and wounded and sixteen hundred prisoners, in addition to which one gun and one British colour were captured. That of the French was as heavy and heavier, amounting to twenty-seven hundred killed and wounded and three hundred prisoners. The struggle was unusually stubborn and murderous, and the fire of the British was so rapid and deadly that three French brigades were almost wiped out of existence.[12] Yet it is said that after this action the hereditary prince would never take British troops under his command again.[13] He admitted that General Waldegrave did wonders in the combat,[14] but he complained of the behaviour of his troops, though Waldegrave bore witness that not a man retired until his ammunition was exhausted.

It may have been that the prince was irritated by the failure of the reserve to arrive when it was wanted; but no blame is imputed to any one for this mischance, which appears to have been due simply to

12. Bourcet.
13. Mauvillon. Yet I find the British Guards with him on the Lippe in 1761.
14. Hereditary prince to Holderness, 19th October 1760.

bad luck. Mauvillon, who is always very frank in his criticism of the British, says flatly that he does not believe in their misconduct on this occasion; and as the only extant list of casualties, though very far from complete, shows that they lost five hundred killed and wounded, it should seem that the prince's strictures were ill deserved. It was hard, too, that he should have forgotten all that they had done for him at Emsdorff and at Warburg, to say nothing of the fact that the heroic charge of the Fifteenth probably saved his force from total destruction at Kloster Kampen itself.

Whether he himself should have hazarded such an action against odds of two to one, with the French bringing up reinforcements from the west, is another question; for it was not as though the fall of Wesel were likely to ensue speedily even if Castries were beaten, while the diversion had proved to be no diversion whatever. On the other hand, the destruction of his corps, or of the best part of it, would have been a severe blow to Ferdinand. Nevertheless the stake, if he should win it, was worth winning; though if he could have foreseen what was immediately before him he would probably have hesitated to play so desperate a game.

After the action he retreated northward to Büderich, to find that the bridge which he had thrown over the Rhine had been swept away by floods, and that he could go no farther. His situation was now desperate, for not only was his retreat cut off, but his ammunition was exhausted. Still, wounded though he was, he faced his difficulties with his usual energy, entrenched himself among his waggons, reconstructed his bridge, and on the 18th crossed the river unmolested, picking up the troops from before Wesel on the eastern bank. Castries followed him as he retreated eastward, thereby forcing him to remain in Westphalia for the protection of Lippstadt and Münster, though the prince none the less made shift to detach a portion of his force to the assistance of Ferdinand.

For to Ferdinand also the failure before Wesel was a serious matter. Any further stroke upon the French was impossible; and the utmost for which he could hope was to drive them out of Hesse and to hold Westphalia safe. He made an effort to expel the French from Göttingen, but without success; and at last, driven to desperation by three months of continuous rain, he cantoned a force in winter-quarters before the town and closed the campaign, leaving the French in possession of Hesse, of the Principality of Göttingen, and of the defiles of Münden, which gave them free ingress into Hanover and Brunswick.

His own headquarters were fixed at Warburg; those of the French at Cassel. Despite all his efforts, superior numbers had told heavily against him; and though he had fired a *feu de joie* for the capture of Montreal, he probably found less consolation in this than in the victories of his master Frederick and at Leignitz and Torgau, (Aug. 15th and Nov. 3rd), in the expulsion of his enemies' forces from Saxony.

CHAPTER 10

Belleisle & Vellinghausen

Meanwhile on the 20th of November, 1760, Parliament had met to hear his first speech from a new king. For on the 25th of October, just before the coming of the news of Kloster Kampen, King George the Second had died suddenly, having lived to see the glories of Queen Anne's reign brought back by Pitt, and the fame of Blenheim and Oudenarde revived not only by Minden and Warburg but by Wandewash and Quebec. George the Third struck a new and strange note in his speech from the throne. "Born and educated in England," he said—and the words were of his own insertion—"I glory in the name of Briton"; and the phrase fell pleasantly on ears that did not love the sound of Hanover; though what this sudden outburst of insular patriotism on the king's part might portend to his German allies was not yet revealed. The estimates for the army were passed with little difficulty, though the Establishment showed a considerable increase. The new regiments that appeared on the list, indeed, were few, for a system had been initiated of raising an indefinite number of independent companies; but these were gradually combined into regiments, and before the campaign opened there was already a corps numbered the hundredth of the Line.[1]

The total number of men voted on the British Establishment was one hundred and four thousand; besides which the embodied militia 1760. was increased from eighteen to twenty-seven thousand, making, together with the troops on the Irish Establishment, over one hundred and forty thousand men raised in the British possessions alone. Adding

---

1. The new regiments were:—Burton's (95th), 10th December 1760; Monson's (96th), 20th January 1761; James Stuart's (97th), 24th January 1761; Grey's (98th), 27th January 1761; Byng's (99th), 16th March 1761; Colin Campbell's (100th), 4th May 1761.

the mercenary forces of Hanover, Hesse, and Brunswick, the number of soldiers in British pay fell little short of two hundred thousand.

Yet for the present no considerable reinforcement was despatched to Ferdinand. A battalion from each regiment of Guards had indeed been sent to him late in the past campaign, together with the usual drafts to fill up vacancies. But Pitt had another enterprise in hand as a diversion in Ferdinand's favour. A scheme of the kind had indeed been on the point of execution in the autumn of 1760; and eight thousand men had actually been embarked for a secret expedition under General Kingsley, but had been returned to the shore on receipt of the news of Kloster Kampen.[2] In January, 1761, however, the same regiments were again warned for service under Major-General Hodgson,[3] and on the 29th of March they sailed from Spithead under convoy of ten ships of the line, besides smaller vessels, under Admiral Keppel, for their unknown destination.[4]

On the 7th of April the fleet anchored off the island of Belleisle on the French coast, and on the following day sailed round it looking for an undefended point. Finally Port La Maria on the south-eastern side was selected; the troops were shifted into flat-bottomed boats, and an attempt was made to storm some French entrenchments which covered the landing-place. But the ground was so steep that only sixty men of the Thirty-Seventh succeeded in making their way to the top of the heights above the sea, and these after a gallant attempt to hold their ground were overpowered by superior numbers. The attempt was therefore abandoned, and the troops were re-embarked, having lost about five hundred men, killed, wounded, and taken. The island was in fact so strong by nature, and so skilfully fortified by art, that Keppel despaired of a successful descent.

The commanders, however, decided that, if feint attacks were made on La Maria and Sauzon some footing might be obtained by ascending the rocks between them, which being judged inaccessible had been left undefended. The attempt was accordingly made on the 22nd and was brilliantly successful. The grenadier company of the Nineteenth contrived to scramble up the rocks and to hold its own on the

2. *Miscellaneous Orders*, 3rd October, 14th November 1760.

3. *Ibid,*, 24th January 1761.

4. The troops were the whole, or detachments, of the 9th, 19th, 30th, 34th, 36th, 67th, 69th, Morgan's (then the 94th), Stuart's (then the 97th), Grey's (then the 98th); two troops of the 16th Light Dragoons, and three companies of Royal Artillery. Detachments of the 3rd, 36th, Crawford's (then 85th) and Boscawen's (then 75th) also arrived in May and June.

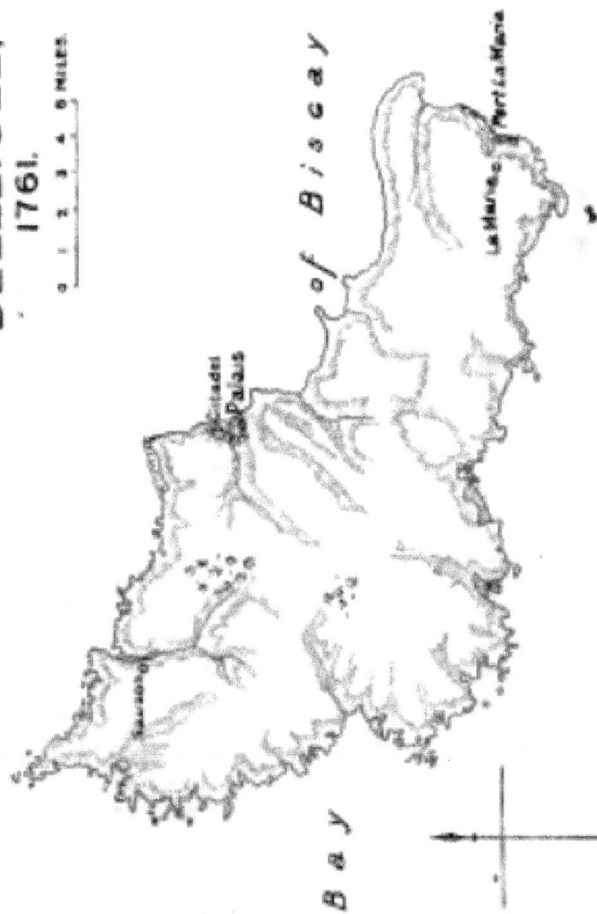

BELLEISLE,
1761.

0 1 2 3 4 5 MILES.

of Biscay

La Maison   Port La Maria

Citadel
Palais

Bay

summit until reinforced, when the men charged with the bayonet, drove back the enemy and captured three guns. The French then retired into the fortress of Palais and proceeded to strengthen the defences; while Hodgson, to his infinite mortification, was obliged to lie idle for a fortnight, being unable to land his heavy artillery owing to continual gales.

At length on the 2nd of May ground was broken, and on the 13th the entrenchments were carried by storm. The French thereupon retired into the citadel, which after a most gallant defence was compelled on the 7th of June to surrender. The losses of the British throughout the whole of the operations were about seven hundred killed and wounded. Thus Belleisle was secured as a place of refreshment for the fleet while engaged in the weary work of blockading the French coast.

Any hopes that might have been built on the value of this expedition as a help to Ferdinand were very speedily dissipated. Ferdinand himself had sought, while it was yet mid-winter, to make good the losses of the past campaign by a bold stroke for the recapture of Hesse. Moving out of his winter-quarters on the 11th of February he distributed his army into three columns. The left or eastern column, under Spörcke, was designed to march to the Werra and Unstrut, and to join with a detachment of Prussians in an attack upon the Saxons in that quarter; the main or central army, under Ferdinand himself, was to march to the Eder; and the right or westward column, which was composed of the troops cantoned in Westphalia under the hereditary prince, was to advance on Fritzlar, while a separate corps was detached to attempt the capture of Marburg.

Spörcke for his part did his work well and gained a brilliant little victory at Langensalza; but the rest of the scheme went to wreck. Broglie on learning of Ferdinand's movements left a garrison in Cassel and retreated first to Hersfeld, behind the Eder, and finally to the Main. But meanwhile the hereditary prince had been delayed for two invaluable days by unexpected resistance at Fritzlar; and Ferdinand, though he had driven the enemy for the moment from Hesse, had left Cassel, Ziegenhain, and Marburg, invested indeed but untaken, behind him. He dared not linger to master these places one after another, for the whole country was laid waste, and the strain of hauling all supplies from the Weser was intolerable. The road from Beverungen to the central column of the army was paved with dead horses, the corpses tracing the whole line of the advance. He was therefore obliged to hasten on to a district where supplies were still obtainable, trusting that good fortune would throw the strong places into his hands before it was too late.

But it was not to be. Broglie quickly concentrated his troops on the Main, summoned twelve thousand men from the Lower Rhine and advanced northward to Giessen; whereupon Ferdinand, who had penetrated as far south as the Ohm, was compelled to fall back to the Eder, (March 20th). On the following day the hereditary prince was attacked by superior numbers at Grünberg and compelled to retreat with loss of two thousand prisoners; and this misfortune neutralised all the advantages so far gained by the enterprise. Ferdinand, therefore, raised the siege of Cassel and fell back with all speed by forced marches; for Broglie had now eighty thousand troops against his own twenty thousand. Arrived at his old position to north of the Diemel he dispersed his troops once more into winter-quarters.

His stroke had failed; and the operations are interesting chiefly as exemplifying the futility, in those days of slow communication, of an advance into an enemy's country, unless at least one fortress were first captured as a place of arms. It is easier to understand the reason for the laborious sieges of Marlborough and Wellington when it is observed that Ferdinand, though he drove the French before him from end to end of Hesse in a few weeks, was obliged to abandon the whole of it and to retreat because he had left Cassel uncaptured in his rear.

The Allies had suffered so terribly from hardship and exposure during this winter's expedition that it was two months before they were again fit to take the field; [5] and the French, partly from the same cause, partly owing to the magnitude of their preparations, needed little less time than they. The Court of Versailles had, in fact, resolved to make a gigantic effort and to close the war forthwith by employment of an overwhelming force. The Army of the Rhine was raised to one hundred thousand men, under the Prince of Soubise, and that of the Main to sixty thousand men under Broglie. Soubise was to advance from the Rhine against Ferdinand early in May; thus forcing the prince either to abandon Westphalia, together with Münster and Lippstadt, in order to gain time for recuperation of his army, or to march with his troops, still weakened and exhausted by the winter's campaign, to fight him.

His task in fact was simply to keep Ferdinand's army in motion

---

5. For example, eight British battalions were by March reduced to a joint total of 700 effective men. Ferdinand to Frederick, 23rd March 1761, Westphalen, v. 220.

until Broglie's troops were refreshed, and ready to advance either into Hanover or to Hameln on the Weser. When Broglie thus occupied the attention of Ferdinand, Soubise would find himself with a free hand in a free field. The weak point of the plan was that the two French armies were to act independently, and that the stronger of them was entrusted to Soubise, an incompetent commander but a favourite with Madame de Pompadour. But in any case the outlook for Ferdinand was formidable, since at the very most he could muster but ninety-three thousand men against one hundred and sixty thousand of the French.

Soubise duly arrived at Frankfort on the 13th of April and summoned Broglie to discuss matters with him. Then, instead of taking the field early in May, he remained motionless behind the Rhine on various pretexts until the beginning of June. Further, he determined, contrary to the advice given to him at Versailles, to pursue operations to the south of the Lippe, and between that river and the Ruhr, in order to effect a junction with Broglie. The motives that may have dictated this resolution are unknown; but it was conjectured that he shrank from engaging so formidable an adversary as Ferdinand without a colleague to share the risk and responsibility.

Meanwhile Ferdinand, selecting the least exhausted of his troops, sent a corps under the hereditary prince to Nottuln, (May 14th), a little to the west of Münster, to watch Soubise, and by great exertions contrived within ten weeks to render both his army and his transport fit to take the field. Soubise's army was known to be encumbered by a vast train of baggage; one troop of Horse Guards, for instance, with a strength of one hundred and forty men, travelling with no fewer than twelve hundred horses attached to it. So all the forage about Münster was destroyed, the inhabitants and their herds being provided for by the king's commissaries, and every step was taken to embarrass the French in their advance to the east.

At length on the 13th of June Soubise crossed the Rhine at Wesel, and arrived ten days later at Unna, a few miles to eastward of Dortmund, where he entrenched himself, with his front to the east. Ferdinand thereupon concentrated his army on the 19th at Paderborn, leaving twenty thousand men under Spörcke on the Diemel to watch Broglie, and a smaller corps of observation before Göttingen. On the 20th he marched westward, and on the 28th encamped over against Soubise, where he was joined by the corps of the hereditary prince. Finding that the French position was too formidable to be attacked, he determined on a bold stroke, (July 1st-2nd), made a forced march of thirty hours round Soubise's left flank by Camen, and appeared suddenly at Dortmund full in his rear and across his line of communication, (July 3rd).

The movement left Soubise free to unite with Broglie; but this was rather an advantage than otherwise to Ferdinand, since the two commanders being on bad terms might neutralise each other, whereas each of them independently was at the head of a stronger army than Ferdinand's. On the 4th of July Ferdinand advanced against the rear of Soubise's camp; whereupon the French general at once moved on, always with the Allies close at his heels, to Soest, (July 6th), where Broglie came to concert with him the junction of the two armies.

Broglie himself had on the 29th of June advanced to the Diemel and obliged Spörcke to abandon Warburg and to retreat, not without loss of part of his artillery. He had then turned westward upon Paderborn, which he had occupied, and thence to Soest, where his army joined that of Soubise on the 10th of July. The joint strength of the two armies at Soest, after deducting the detachments made from both of them, was just about one hundred thousand men. Ferdinand's force, after the arrival of Spörcke, who had made his way to him from the Diemel with all haste, amounted to no more than sixty thousand men. Even with such odds against him, however, Ferdinand stood firm, refusing to cross to the north bank of the Lippe and abandon Lippstadt, as the French commanders had hoped. He was determined that they should fight him for Lippstadt; and they, knowing their adversary, were not too eager to hazard the venture.

After sundry small changes and shiftings of position between the 7th and 11th of July Ferdinand made the following dispositions. General von Spörcke with about eight thousand men was left on the north bank of the Lippe at Hersfeld, to watch Prince Xavier of Saxony, who lay with a corps in the vicinity of Paderborn. The main army was encamped on the south bank of the Lippe, with its left resting on the river; from whence the left wing extended to the village of Kirchdünckern on the Ase, a brook impassable except by bridges. Vellinghausen, Ferdinand's headquarters, lay midway between the Ase and the Lippe at the foot of a declivity called the Dünckerberg. From the Lippe to Vellinghausen the ground was occupied by Wutgenau's corps, of seven battalions and five squadrons, all of them German troops.

From Vellinghausen to Kirchdünckern the heights were held by Granby's corps, consisting of two battalions of British grenadiers, the Fifth, Twelfth, Twenty-Fourth and Thirty-Seventh Foot under Briga-

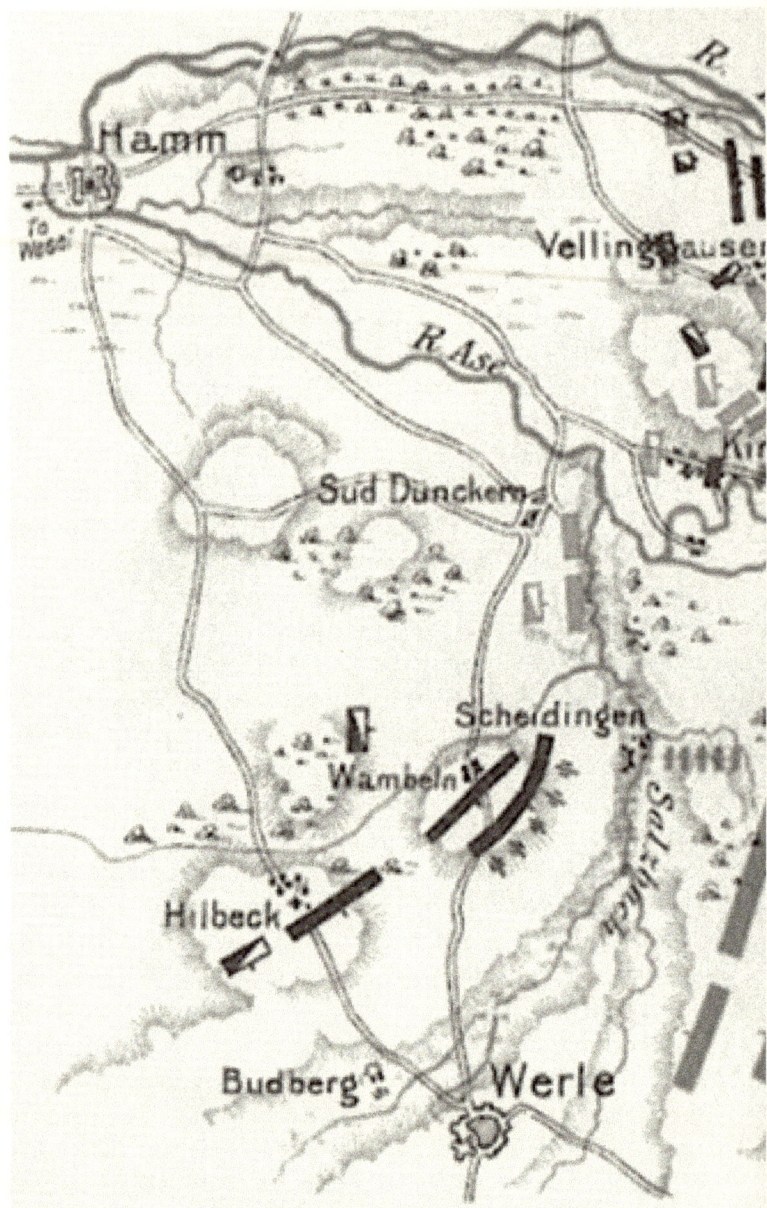

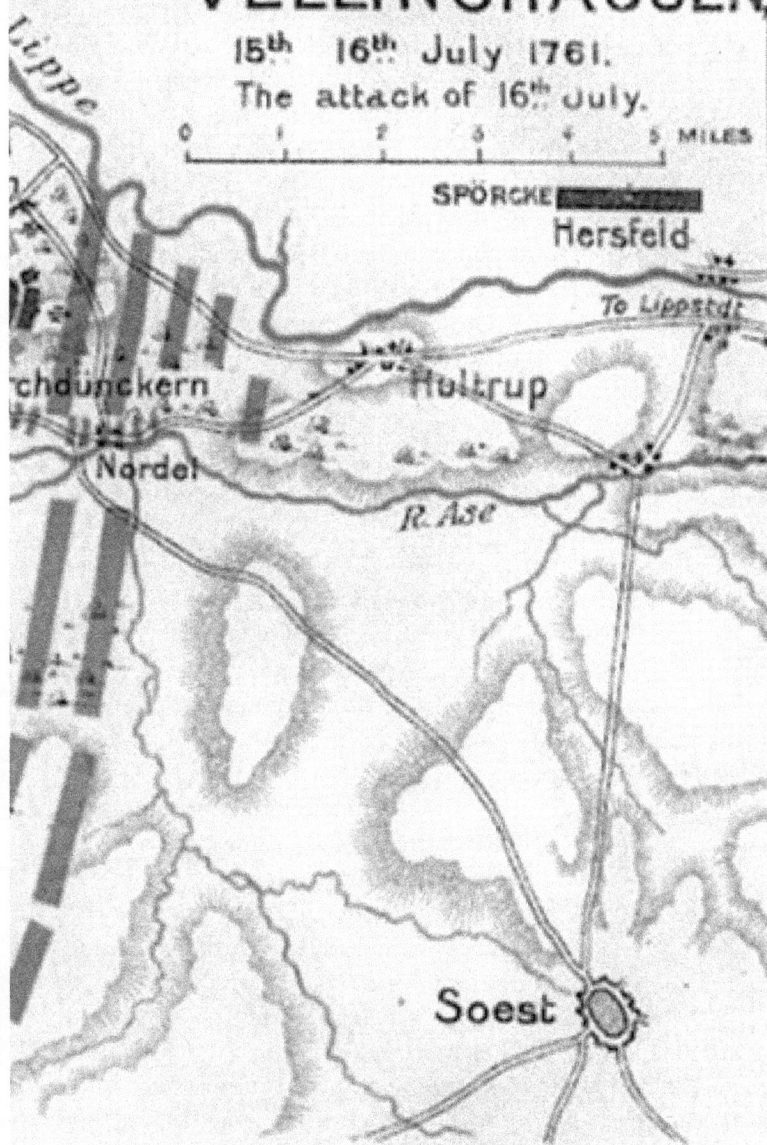

VELLINGHAUSEN.

15th 16th July 1761.

The attack of 16th July.

0   1   2   3   4   5 MILES

SPÖRCKE ▆▆▆▆▆

Hersfeld

To Lippstdt

...chdünckern

Holtrup

Nordel

R. Ase

Lippe

Soest

dier Sandford, Keith's and Campbell's Highlanders, six foreign battalions, the Greys, Seventh and Eleventh Dragoons in one brigade under General Harvey, and eight foreign squadrons, together with a regiment of Hanoverian artillery.

From the Ase the position was prolonged to the right along a similar line of heights by the villages of Sud Dünckern and Wambeln to the rear of Werle at Budberg, the whole of the front being covered by a marshy brook called the Salzbach. From the Ase to Wambeln the ground was occupied by Anhalt's corps of ten German battalions and the First, Sixth, and Tenth British Dragoons; to the right of Anhalt stood Conway's corps, of three battalions of British Guards with their grenadiers massed into a fourth battalion, Townsend's brigade of the Eighth, Twentieth, Twenty-Fifth, and Fiftieth Foot, and the First, Third, and Seventh Dragoon Guards; to the right of Conway stood Howard's corps, consisting of Cavendish's brigade of the Eleventh, Twenty-Fifth, Twenty-Third, and Fifty-First Foot, two German battalions, the British light batteries and two brigades of Hessian artillery; and finally the extreme right from Wambeln to Hilbeck was held by the hereditary prince's corps of twenty-five battalions and twenty-four squadrons of Germans.

The Salzbach was an obstacle well-nigh insuperable, the only passage by which the French could cross it being by the village of Scheidingen, opposite to Conway's corps, where an old redoubt, dating from the days of Turenne, still remained to bar the way. The weak point of the position was its right flank which, though more or less protected by marshy ground, lay practically in the air, and could have been turned with little difficulty.

The plan of the French commanders, though it took no advantage of this defect, was not ill conceived. Broglie was to attack the corps of Wutgenau and Granby, but particularly that of Granby between the Lippe and the Ase, with his whole force; while Soubise kept the rest of the Allies distracted by an attack on Scheidingen, at the same time sending a cloud of light troops round the right flank of the Allies to Hamm, five miles in their rear, so as to create confusion and embarrass their retreat. The attack was fixed for the 13th but was deferred for two days; and it was not until the evening of the 15th that Ferdinand was apprised of the advance of the French in force against his left. For some reason Wutgenau's corps had been encamped a thousand yards in rear of its position in the line of battle; and although it had received orders at noon, in consequence of suspicious movements by the French, to strike tents and march forward, yet this order had been cancelled.

Thus Broglie's attack came upon it as a complete surprise. Granby's corps had only just time to seize its arms and turn out, leaving the tents standing; the Highlanders indeed hardly emerging from their tents before the French guns opened fire on them. Yet there was no confusion, and Granby's dispositions were so good that he was able to hold his own till Wutgenau's troops came up. The two corps then made a fine defence until darkness put an end to the combat; but none the less the French had succeeded in taking Nordel, a village on Granby's right front, and had made good their footing in Vellinghausen.

Meanwhile Soubise had not yet moved forward against Scheidingen. The time fixed by the marshals for their decisive attack has been, in fact, the early hours of the 16th, so that Broglie's advance had been premature. He excused himself by saying that he had intended only to drive in the outposts of the Allies, but that he had been encouraged by his unexpected success to bring forward more troops to hold the ground that he had gained, and that he had accordingly appealed to Soubise to hasten his movements likewise. Had Broglie really pushed his attack home he would probably have succeeded, for the Allies were too weak to stop him and were, moreover, short of ammunition. But the marshal was too timid a man to take responsibility on his own shoulders; so instead of making a bold attempt to carry the Dünckerberg, which if successful must have forced Ferdinand to retreat, he stopped short at Vellinghausen, leaving the Allies in their position unmoved.

The night passed uneasily in the Allied camp. Between the Lippe and the Ase skirmishing never ceased. The road to Hamm was full of waggons going and returning with loads of ammunition; Anhalt's corps, together with all the British of Howard's corps, was streaming across the Ase to reinforce Granby; and Conway's and the hereditary prince's were extending themselves leftward to cover the ground thus left vacant. For Ferdinand knew Broglie to be his most dangerous antagonist, and was determined to stop him at all costs by fresh troops. Broglie, on his side, was equally busy replacing the battalions that had already been engaged; and the dawn was no sooner come than his columns deployed and attacked in earnest.

The ground was so much broken up by hedges and ditches that in many places the troops engaged, though no more than one hundred and fifty yards apart, were unable to see each other, and fired furiously,

JOHN MANNERS, MARQUIS OF GRANBY

not without destructive effect, at every puff of smoke that betrayed an enemy's presence. From four until eight o'clock this fusillade continued, neither side gaining or losing an inch of ground, until at last it slackened from the sheer exhaustion of the men, after more than twelve hours of intermittent action.

Meanwhile Broglie looked anxiously for Soubise's demonstration against the Allied centre and right, but he looked in vain. Soubise, though he did indeed bring forward troops against Scheidingen, made but a faint attack, often renewed with unchangeable feebleness and as often repulsed. Then after half an hour's respite, the fire opened again on the Allied left. Spörcke had detached six battalions to Wutgenau from Hersfeld; and the arrival of fresh troops infused new life into the engagement. Broglie too showed symptoms of reviving energy, for two French batteries were observed in motion towards a height opposite the Dünckerberg, from which they might have made havoc of Granby's corps.

Ferdinand ordered that the height should be carried at all costs; and Maxwell's grenadiers, Keith's and Campbell's Highlanders and four foreign battalions advanced forthwith to storm it. The French were so much exhausted that they appear hardly to have awaited the attack. They broke and fled precipitately, abandoning their dead, their wounded, and several guns. Maxwell's grenadiers alone made four battalions prisoners; and Broglie, disheartened by his failure and by the apathy of Soubise, gave the word to retreat. The ground was too much broken for the action of cavalry; so he was able to draw off his troops with little loss indeed, but not without shame and disgrace.

Thus ended the Battle of Vellinghausen, one of the feeblest ever fought by the French Army. The losses were not great on either side for the numbers engaged. Those of the French were reckoned at from five to six thousand men, besides eight colours and nineteen guns; those of the Allies did not reach the figure of sixteen hundred men, of whom over nine-tenths belonged to the corps to the north of the Ase. The brunt of the fighting fell of course on Granby's troops; but the casualties of the British with him little exceeded four hundred men, while those of the British in other parts of the field did not amount to fifty.

The victory was in fact trifling except for its moral effects; but these were sufficient. The French were humbled at the failure of a hundred thousand men against fifty thousand; and Broglie and Soubise, who had left the camp with embraces, returned to it sworn enemies, each bitterly reproaching the other for the loss of the battle. Lastly, Broglie, who possessed some military talent and had hitherto been anxious to bring his enemy to action, came to the conclusion that a general engagement with Ferdinand was a thing henceforth not to be courted but to be shunned.

The remainder of the campaign is reckoned to be the finest example of Ferdinand's skill as a general; but it is impossible in this place to sketch it in more than the faintest outline. After the action, Soubise made up Broglie's army to forty thousand men, and therewith the two commanders separated; Broglie marching on Paderborn, (July 27th), for operations against Hanover and Hesse, while Soubise made for Wesel to threaten Westphalia. The hereditary prince was detached to follow Soubise and to harass his rear-guard, while Ferdinand marched some thirty miles eastward to Büren, to be ready to move into Hesse and threaten Broglie's communications with Frankfort.

At the same time Granby's corps was sent forward to Stadtberg, to drive back a French corps under Stainville, which covered Hesse at the line of the Diemel. At Büren Ferdinand remained, with his eye always on Lippstadt, until the 10th of August; when, Stainville having been forced back to Cassel and Soubise to the Rhine, both at a safe distance from the precious fortress on the Lippe, he marched away to keep watch over Broglie's army.

That officer had used his time to advance to Höxter, aiming at the capture of Hameln and the mastery of the line of the Weser, and had detached a corps under Prince Xavier of Saxony into the Principality of Göttingen. Ferdinand by swift marches brought his army to northward of Broglie's at Reilenkirchen, (Aug. 16th), thus heading him back from Hameln; while a separate corps, which he had sent across the Weser, attacked the French detachments about Göttingen. The hereditary prince, finding nothing to fear from Soubise, also returned from the Rhine to threaten Broglie from the south. The marshal thereupon crossed the Weser; and Ferdinand, for all his unwillingness to move to the east bank of the river, perforce followed him, (Aug 22nd); carefully avoiding an engagement, however, lest Soubise should seize the opportunity to march on Lippstadt.

Soubise, finding himself unwatched, moved eastward again towards Hanover; whereupon the hereditary prince flew back to look after him, and Ferdinand retiring with the rest of the army to the Diemel, advanced against Broglie's communications with Marburg and Frankfort, (Aug. 28th). This movement brought Broglie back hurriedly to Cassel; whereupon Ferdinand retired quietly to Geismar on the Diemel, having accomplished his object of occupying Broglie's attention for weeks and of rendering his movements absolutely purposeless, without the risk of an action.

It was a whole fortnight before Broglie ventured to return to the east side of the Weser, having meanwhile reinforced Stainville's army for the protection of Hesse, and furnished him with most careful instructions for his guidance. No sooner was the marshal's back turned, than Ferdinand made a sudden dash upon Stainville, (Sept. 20th), just to south of the Diemel, and though he failed to inflict any great damage on him, forced him to retire to Cassel and brought Broglie back in all haste from Hanover. Meanwhile the lethargic Soubise had made a diversion towards the sea, had actually taken Emden, and was threatening Bremen. The hereditary prince was as usual despatched to hunt him back to the Rhine; and Ferdinand's communications with Holland were restored.

There still remained some weeks, however, before the campaign could be closed; and Broglie, despite all Ferdinand's activity, was strong enough to detach a corps under Prince Xavier into Brunswick, (Oct. 10th), which captured Wolfenbüttel and bade fair to capture Brunswick itself. The loss of these two fortresses would have been serious, since the French could have turned them into bases of operations for the next campaign, when Ferdinand would have found it impossible to attend both to Brunswick and to Lippstadt. He therefore hastened northward at once from the Diemel to save his brother's capital; whereupon Prince Xavier, though Ferdinand had travelled no further than Hameln on his way, at once withdrew from before Brunswick and evacuated Wolfenbüttel.

Much relieved at the news of this deliverance, Ferdinand halted at Hameln until November, when Soubise went into winter-quarters. He then made a final effort to drive Broglie from the eastern bank of the Weser, but succeeded only in thrusting him back for a short distance from his northernmost post at Einbeck. Broglie then went into winter-quarters along the Leine from Göttingen to Nordheim, and the Allies followed his example; their chain of posts running from Münster along the line of the Lippe and Diemel, and eastward through the Sollinger Forest to Ferdinand's headquarters at Hildesheim.

So ended this most arduous campaign, in which, though overmatched by two to one, Ferdinand had won a victory on the battlefield and lost little or no territory. The exertion demanded from his troops by incessant and severe marches told heavily upon their efficiency, and the more so since many of the men had been already much weakened by the winter's campaign in Hesse. The waste of the army was in fact appalling, amounting to no fewer than five-and-twenty thousand out of ninety-five thousand men. Of these some few had been killed in action, considerably more had deserted, still more had been invalided, and fully one-half had died of hardship and disease.

It was only at such a price that Ferdinand could make one army do the work of two; and the task would have been beyond even his ability had not one of the commanders matched against him been utterly incompetent, and the other hampered by constant interference from Versailles. The extreme laxity of discipline among the French also helped him not a little, and served to heighten the moral superiority of his own troops. But, making all such allowance in his favour, the campaign remains memorable in the annals of war for the consummate skill with which Ferdinand kept two armies, jointly of double his strength, continually in motion for six months, without permitting them to reap the slightest advantage from their operations.

CHAPTER 11

Wilhelmsthal

Before the campaign closed in Germany, the great minister who had revealed to England for the first time the plenitude of her strength in arms, and had turned that strength to such mighty enterprises, was fallen from power. The accession of the new king had brought with it a steady increase in the ascendency of John, Earl of Bute, long a trusted member of his household and now his chief adviser and friend. Blameless in private life and by no means lacking in culture or accomplishments, Bute was both in council and debate a man of distressing mediocrity. Possessing neither sense of the ridiculous nor knowledge of his own limitations, and exalted by mere accident to a position of great influence, he interpreted the caprice of fortune as the reward of merit and aimed at once at the highest office.

He was, in fact, one of the many men who, finding it no great exertion to climb up the winding stairs of a cathedral tower, press on, ducking, stooping, and crawling to the top, to find when they reach it that they dare not look down. Being weak as well as ambitious he was compelled to fall back on intrigue in default of ability to help him upward, and having succeeded in displacing Lord Holderness as Secretary of State in March 1761, he turned next to the ousting of Pitt himself. The opportunity soon came.

The French Court, weary of the war, approached Pitt with proposals for peace. Resolved, as he said, that no Peace of Utrecht should again sully the annals of England, Pitt not only made large demands for the benefit of Britain, but insisted that even a separate peace between Britain and France should not deter King George from giving aid to the King of Prussia. Curiously enough the negotiation was broken off owing precisely to one of the most disgraceful concessions made at the Peace of Utrecht. The Bourbon King of Spain, Charles the Third, who had succeeded to the throne in 1759, cultivated the friendship of the Bourbon King of France; and the result was a secret treaty of alliance between them, which presently became famous as the Family Compact. Pitt no sooner obtained an inkling of this agreement than he put an end to negotiations with France, and advocated immediate declaration of war against Spain.

As shall presently be seen, he made his preparations, which were effective enough; but above all he desired to strike at Spain while she was still unready for war. The Cabinet, however, was alarmed at so bold a measure, being too blind to see that in such a case aggression is the truest precaution. Many of the ministry had only with difficulty been persuaded to second Pitt in the lofty language which he had held towards France; and Bute, who abhorred all interference with affairs on the Continent, was a leader among the dissentients. Lord Temple alone stood by his great chief, so Pitt, unable to prevail, resigned, and his solitary supporter with him. All power passed into the hands of Bute; and within three months Spain, having gained the time that she needed for her military preparations, (Jan. 4th 1762), assumed so offensive a tone that Bute, as Pitt had predicted, was to his huge vexation obliged to declare war against her himself. Such is the fashion in which politicians make difficulties for generals.

Fortunately the designs of Pitt for the new year against both France and Spain were fully matured, and the means of executing them were ready to hand. In June two new regiments [1] had been either raised or formed out of existing independent companies, and thirteen more had been added in August and October,[2] thus bringing the number of regiments of the Line up to one hundred and fifteen.

The total number of men voted by Parliament for 1762 was little short of one hundred and fifty thousand men, making with the German mercenaries a total of two hundred and fifteen thousand men in

1. Johnston's (101st), Wedderburn's (102nd).
2. Oswald's (103rd), 10th August 1761; Tonyn's (104th), 10th August 1761; Graeme's (105th), 15th October 1761; Barré's (106th), 17th October 1761; Beauclerk's (107th), 16th October 1761; Macdougall's (108th), 17th October 1761; Nairn's (109th), 13th October 1761; Deakin's (110th), 14th October 1761; Markham's (112th), 16th October 1761; Hamilton's (113th), 17th October 1761; McLean's (114th), 18th October 1761; Crawford's (115th), 19th October 1761. The lists in the Army List and in the Miscellaneous Orders do not quite correspond. According to the former the 108th was John Scott's, and the 111th Warkworth's, both bearing date April 1762. But there was a corps formed under Macdougall as above, and another under Colonel Ogle in October 1761, which I take to be the 108th and 111th respectively.

British pay. There were thus men in abundance for any enterprise; and the sphere of operations had been marked out by Pitt.

Yet another expedition brought the British face to face with their new enemy on more familiar ground than Luzon. The Spaniards, on the pretext of Portuguese friendship with England, in April invaded Portugal, overran the country as far as the Douro from the north, and threw another force against Almeida from the east. The injured kingdom appealed to England for help; and in May orders were sent to Belleisle for the despatch of four regiments of infantry,[3] together with the detachment of the Sixteenth Light Dragoons, to Portugal. Two more regiments were added from Ireland,[4] bringing the total up to about seven thousand men; and simultaneously a number of British officers were sent to take up commands in the Portuguese Army. Unfortunately there was some trouble over the selection of a commander; and though the two regiments from Ireland were actually in the Tagus by the first week in May, it was not until June that the rest of the troops arrived, with the Count of Lippe Bückeburg, the famous artillerist, as Commander-in-Chief of the Allied forces, and Lord Loudoun in command of the British.

The operations that followed were so trifling and of so short duration that they are unworthy of detailed mention. The Spaniards captured Almeida early in August; and Bückeburg was obliged to stand on the defensive and cover Lisbon at the line of the Tagus. Two brilliant little affairs, however, served to lift an officer, who so far was little known, into a prominence which was one day to be disastrous to himself and to England. This was Brigadier-General John Burgoyne, Colonel of the Sixteenth Light Dragoons, who with four hundred troopers of his regiment surprised the town of Valencia de Alcantara after a forced march of forty-five miles, annihilated a regiment of Spanish infantry and captured several prisoners (Aug. 26th).

Not content with this, he a month later surprised the camp of another party of Spaniards at Villa Velha, on the south bank of the Tagus, dispersed, it with considerable loss and captured six guns, at a cost of but one man killed and ten wounded. Such affairs, which in Ferdinand's army were so common as seldom to be noticed, made Burgoyne and the Sixteenth [5] the heroes of this short campaign; but

---

3. 3rd, 67th, Boscawen's, Crawford's.

4. Armstrong's, Blayney's.

5. On one occasion a sergeant and six men of this regiment killed or captured every man of a party of five-and-twenty Spanish horse under an officer.

Sielen

Corbeke

Desenberg

Warburg

Liebenau

$\mathbf{V^d}$ FERDINAND

Hofgeismar

Gröbenste

Wilda

MAIN A...

Kall

Volks &
marsen

ADVANCE OF GRANBY

Wilhelmsth

Zierenburg

WILHELMSTHAL,

24ᵗʰ June 1762.

*Dispositions at the opening
of the attack of the Allies.*

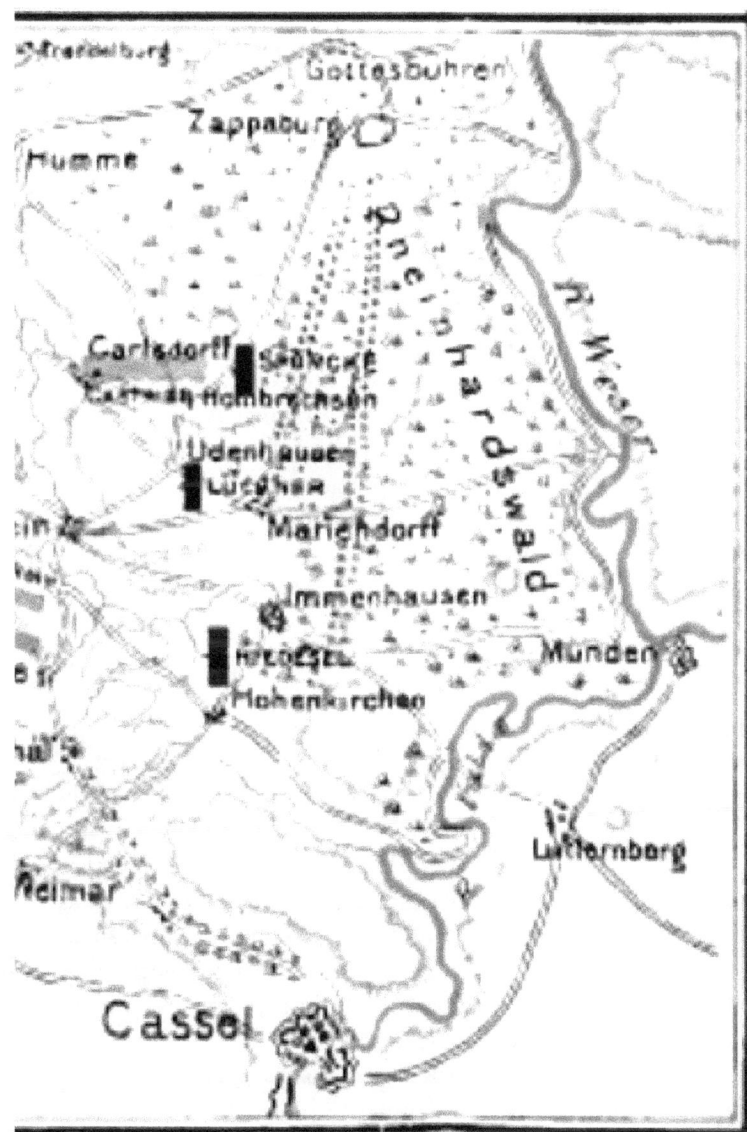

though the regiment has lived the rest of its life according to this beginning, Burgoyne's career will end twenty years hence at Saratoga.

From these scattered enterprises against Spain I return to Ferdinand's last campaign against the old enemy in Germany. We left the contending parties in their winter-quarters, the French Army of the Rhine cantoned along the river from Cleve to Cologne; the Army of the Main extending from Altenkirchen, a little to north of Treves, north-eastward to Cassel and from Cassel south-eastward to Langensalza; and the Allies, facing almost due south, stretched from Münster to Halberstadt. The whole situation was, however, changed in various respects. The French had resolved to throw their principal strength into the Army of the Main, which was accordingly raised to eighty thousand men under the command of Soubise and Marshal d'Estrées; Broglie having been recalled to France.

The Army of the Rhine was reduced proportionately to thirty thousand men under the Prince of Condé. The total numbers of the French, though less than in previous years, still remained far superior to Ferdinand's; but, on the other hand, owing to the change of ministry in England and the reopening of negotiations by Bute, the Court of Versailles was content to hold the ground already gained without attempt at further conquest. Soubise and d'Estrées were therefore instructed to cling fast to Cassel and Göttingen, to spare the district between the Rhine and the Lahn with a view to winter-quarters, and to destroy the forage between the Eder and the Diemel so as to prevent Ferdinand from manoeuvring on their flanks and rear.

Ferdinand on his side, though still outmatched by the armies opposed to him, was relatively stronger in numbers than in any previous year, having a nominal total of ninety-five thousand men ready for the field. Winter-quarters were little disturbed during the early months of 1762, the country having been so much devastated that neither side could move, from lack of forage, until the green corn was already grown high. Towards the end of May both armies began to concentrate; and Ferdinand, though much delayed by the negligence of the British Ministry in recruiting the British regiments to their right strength, determined to be first in the field.

Having detached a strong corps under the hereditary prince to watch the movements of Condé, (June 18th), he concentrated at Brakel, a little to the east of Paderborn, and advanced to the Diemel, where he posted the main army about Corbeke, with Granby's corps to westward of it at Warburg. Hearing at the same time that the French had left a corps under Prince Xavier on the east of the Weser to invade Hanover, he detached General Lückner with a small force across the river to keep an eye on him, sending also parties to seize the Castle of Zappaburg, some few miles to south-east, to secure communications with Lückner, and to occupy the passes leading from the south of the Diemel into Hesse.

Meanwhile, on the 22nd of June, Soubise and d'Estrées moved northward from Cassel with the main body of the army as far as Gröbenstein, fixed their headquarters at Wilhelmsthal and halted. The design of this movement is unintelligible unless, as is conjectured by one writer, (Mauvillon), they wished simply to amuse themselves at the castle of Wilhelmsthal; but in any case they neglected all necessary precautions. Their right flank rested on the large forest known as the Reinhardswald, and might have been rendered absolutely secure by the occupation of the Zappaburg, which commanded every road through that forest; yet they had suffered this important post to fall into Ferdinand's hands.

Again, the occupation of the passes to the south of the Diemel would have secured their front; but here also they had allowed the Allies to be before them. None the less there they remained, careless of all consequences, at Wilhelmsthal; while to tempt an active enemy still farther, they stationed a corps under M. de Castries before their right front at Carlsdorff, in absolute isolation from their main body. Ferdinand saw his opportunity, and though he could bring but fifty thousand men against their seventy thousand, resolved to strike at once.

On the 23rd he recalled Lückner from across the Weser to Gottesbühren, a little to the north of the Zappaburg; and on hearing of his safe arrival at eight o'clock of the same evening, ordered the whole army to be under arms at midnight. For Lückner's corps was but one of the toils which he was preparing to draw around the Unsuspecting French; and the places for the rest had already been chosen. Spörcke, with twelve battalions of Hanoverians and several squadrons, was to advance from the left of the main body, turn a little to the eastward upon Humme after crossing the Diemel, and, marching from thence southward, was to fall upon the right flank and rear of Castries' corps at Hombrechsen.

Lückner, with six battalions and seven squadrons, was to march south-west from Gottesbühren through the Zappaburg to Udenhausen, and form up to the left of Spörcke on Castries' right rear. Colonel Riedesel was to push forward from the Zappaburg with a body of irregulars to Hohenkirch, on the south and left of Lückner. Meanwhile Ferdinand was to advance with the main body in five columns between Liebenau and Sielen, upon the front of the French principal army, while Granby should move south upon Zierenberg and fall upon its left flank. Supposing that every corps fulfilled its duty exactly in respect of time and place, there was good hope that the entire force of the French might be destroyed.

Riedesel and Lückner were punctually in their appointed places at seven o'clock on the morning of the 24th. Spörcke's two columns, on emerging from the Reinhardswald at five o'clock, found only two vedettes before them on the heights of Hombrechsen, and ascended those heights unopposed. Then, however, not seeing Castries' corps, which, as it chanced, was hidden from them by a wood, they turned to their left instead of to their right, and advanced unconsciously towards the front of the French main army. The startled vedettes galloped back to give the alarm; and Castries hurriedly calling his men to arms prepared to retreat. Pushing forward his cavalry right and left to screen his movements from Spörcke and from Riedesel, Castries quickly set his infantry in order for march; and having contrived to hold Spörcke at bay for an hour, began his retreat upon Wilhelmsthal and Cassel.

Lückner came up as he had been bidden at Udenhausen, but meeting part of Spörcke's corps on its march in the wrong direction was fired upon by it; and in the confusion Castries was able to make his escape. Riedesel being weak in numbers could not stop him, though he fell furiously with his hussars upon the rear-guard and cut one regiment of French infantry to pieces; but except for this loss Castries retired with little damage. Thus, as so often happens, failed the most important detail of Ferdinand's elaborate combinations.

Meanwhile the French main army, startled out of its sleep by the sound of the guns about Hombrechsen, was in absolute confusion. Fortunately for the Marshals, the unlucky mistake as to Lückner's corps which had saved Castries, saved them also, since it checked Spörcke's advance against their right. Breaking up their camp with amazing rapidity, they formed upon the heights and hastened their baggage away towards Cassel. Lückner, awake to the miscarriage of the turning movement on the French right, now begged Kielmansegge, who commanded the left column of Spörcke's corps, to hasten with him to Hohenkirchen, from whence a cross way to westward would enable them to bar every road between Wilhelmsthal and Cassel. But Kielmansegge persisted in attacking the right flank of the French main body, despite the fact that it was covered by a brook running through a swampy valley; and before he could effect his passage over this obstacle, the opportunity for cutting off the French retreat was lost.

Meanwhile the troops under Ferdinand in the centre advanced against the French front, though very slowly. Spörcke's right column formed up on their left, but being out of its right place hampered the advance of the rest and caused lamentable delay. The French main army, having cleared its baggage out of the way, was falling back in several columns towards Wilhelmsthal, when the appearance of Granby on their left showed them the full extent of their peril. The flower of the French infantry was then collected under M. de Stainville and thrown out on the left to cover the retreat of the main body at any cost; and now the action began in earnest. Taking up a strong position in a wood Stainville prepared to do his utmost. Granby's infantry consisted of three battalions of British Guards, the British grenadiers in three battalions, and the Fifth and Eighth Foot,—some of the finest troops in the British Army—but the fight was long and stubborn.

Stainville appears at first to have taken the offensive and to have fallen upon the head of Granby's columns before the whole of his troops had come up, but to have been gradually forced back as more and more of the British battalions advanced into action. French and English came to close quarters, guns were taken and retaken, and for a time two British cannon remained in the hands of the French. Granby, however, seems to have got the upper hand at last, to have surrounded the wood on two sides and to have made his dispositions for surrounding it on all sides, when Ferdinand's troops at last came up on Stainville's rear and put an end to the conflict. The gallant Frenchman's corps was nearly annihilated; fifteen hundred men were killed and wounded, nearly three thousand surrendered to the Fifth Foot alone,[6] and two battalions only made good their escape. The Allied Army advanced a little to the south of Wilhelmsthal; and so the action came to an end.

The losses of the Allies were small, reaching but seven hundred men killed and wounded, of which four hundred and fifty belonged to Granby's corps. The result of the action was in fact a great disappointment, due partly to the mistakes of Spörcke and Kielmansegge,

---

6. The Fifth, having captured a large body of French grenadiers, received the privilege of wearing French grenadiers' caps, which were modified later into the fusilier-caps, which they still wear. They also bear the name of Wilhelmsthal on their colours.

partly to the extreme slowness of Ferdinand's advance in the centre. The main body of the Allies indeed seems to have taken five hours to move from Gröbenstein to Wilhelmsthal, a distance of little more than four miles; and the fact would appear to indicate considerable clumsiness on the part of some officer or officers in the handling of their men. Still the fact remained that forty thousand men had attacked seventy thousand and driven them back in confusion; and the French were not a little shamefaced and discouraged over their defeat.

On the night of the action Soubise and d'Estrées fell back across the Fulda and took up a position between Cassel and Lutternberg. Ferdinand therefore ordered Granby's corps to a position near Cassel and sent forward a detachment to clear the enemy from the north bank of the Eder; whereupon the French evacuated Fritzlar and retiring across the Fulda took post upon its eastern bank. Both armies remained in this position until the 1st of July, Ferdinand trying always to force the French back, but obliged to act with caution, since Prince Xavier's Saxons had joined the French at Lutternberg and might at any time give trouble on the eastern side of the Weser. Finally on the 24th he boldly attacked the French right at Lutternberg and completely defeated it.[7] The French thereupon fell back to Melsungen on the Fulda, while Ferdinand took up a position opposite to them on the western bank of the river and threatened their communications with Frankfort.

The marshals then summoned Condé from the Rhine, but Ferdinand continued to press their communications so hard that at length they evacuated Göttingen and retreated by Hersfeld and Fulda to Vilbel, a little to the north of Frankfort; Ferdinand marching parallel with them on their western flank to the Nidda, in the hope, which was disappointed, of preventing their junction with Condé. So far he had done well, for he had for the present driven the French armies from Hesse.

Meanwhile Condé, obedient to orders, had marched towards Frankfort, joining Soubise a little to the south of Friedberg on the 30th of August. The hereditary prince, who had followed him closely all the way from the Rhine, attacked him on the same day, apparently in ignorance of the presence of Soubise's army, and was repulsed with considerable loss. For the next few days the two armies remained inactive, Ferdinand between the Nidder and Nidda with his headquarters at Staden, facing south-west, and the French opposite to him

---

7. No British troops were engaged in this combat.

between Friedburg and Butzbach. Such a position, while forces were so unequal, could not continue long; and on the 7th of September the French moved northward by Giessen towards the Eder. Ferdinand, divining that their design was to cut him off from Cassel, which it was his own intention to besiege, at once hurried northward to stop them.

It was a race between the two armies. The French travelled due north by Giessen and Marburg, crossing the Lahn above the latter town. Ferdinand made for Homberg on the north bank of the Ohm, and turning north-westward from thence marched on by Kirchhain and Wetter, where he overtook the French advanced guard. On the following day, (Sept. 15th), he offered battle; but Soubise declined, and, turning to the right about, repassed the Lahn and encamped along the line of the Ohm, with his left at Marburg and his right over against Homberg. Ferdinand thereupon took post in full sight of the enemy on the opposite bank of the river, with his left at Homberg and his right extended beyond Kirchhain. This was the position from which he had intended Imhoff to cover Hesse in 1760; and he had no intention now of allowing the French to break through it to Cassel, for he had made up his mind to recover Cassel for himself.

The valley of the Ohm south-eastward from Kirchhain is about eleven hundred yards broad, rising gradually on the east bank of the river to a height called the Galgenberg, and on the western bank to a steep basaltic hill known as the Amöneberg. The Ohm itself between these hills is from twenty to thirty feet wide and from five to seven feet deep, flowing between steep banks. Just to the south of the Amöneberg was a stone bridge by which stood a water-mill, consisting of a massive court with a group of houses. The steep sides of the Amöneberg frown close to it on the northern hand; but to westward the ground rises in a gentle slope, through which a hollow road, covered by an old redoubt, ran down to the mill.

The town and castle of the Amöneberg itself was surrounded with a wall and towers strong enough, on the south and south-western sides, to defy all but heavy artillery. The bridge with the mill and the castle beyond it were for some reason neglected by the Allies. There had been some attempt to secure the bridge itself, and a redoubt had been begun on Ferdinand's side of the river for its defence; but the breastwork was not above three feet high and as many feet thick, so that it could be commanded by an enemy's fire, and the more easily since the western or French bank of the river was the higher.

159

The court of the mill was occupied by but thirteen men; the old redoubt appears not to have been occupied at all; and the garrison of the castle of Amöneberg consisted of a single battalion of irregulars only. Yet the Amöneberg was an advanced post over against the enemy's left wing and on the enemy's side of the river; and the possession of the bridge was of vital importance to the Allies, not only to ensure communication with that advanced post, but to bar the advance of the French across the Ohm and to secure to Ferdinand the means of taking the offensive. The carelessness which allowed these points to remain so slenderly guarded is therefore almost inexplicable.

The French were not slow to take advantage of the opening thus afforded to them. On the night of the 20th they invested the castle of the Amöneberg so closely that not a man of the garrison could pass through their lines, and, driving the thirteen men from the mill, occupied the court as well as the old redoubt with light troops. This done they waited till morning, and at six o'clock, under cover of a dense mist, opened a heavy fire on the bridge and on the unfinished redoubt beyond it. The men in that redoubt, two hundred Hanoverians, resisted stoutly, in order to gain time for their supports to come up and for their artillery on the Galgenberg to answer the French batteries. The corps in occupation of the ground immediately before the Brückemühle (for so the mill was named) was Zastrow's of seven battalions, seven squadrons and six guns; while Wangenheim's corps of about the same strength lay on his left, and Granby's[8] on the heights of Kirchhain to his right.

Ferdinand on hearing the sound of the firing hastened to the scene of action and found the redoubt still safe, the two hundred Hanoverians having held it stubbornly for two hours until relieved by Zastrow. But meanwhile the French brought forward more guns behind the veil of the mist; and presently thirty pieces of cannon were playing furiously upon the redoubt, while the infantry under cover of the fire renewed their attack on the bridge. Zastrow continued to feed the redoubt with fresh troops, and so held his ground; but the full significance of the attack was not realised until at ten o'clock the mist rolled away, when it was seen by the French dispositions that the enemy was bent upon carrying the bridge at any cost. Then at last Ferdinand ordered up Granby's corps from Kirchhain to Zastrow's assistance.

Meanwhile the fight waxed hotter. The superiority of the French

8. Three battalions of British Guards, three battalions of British grenadiers, two of Highlanders, the Blues, and 1st Dragoon Guards.

in artillery made itself felt; nine out of twelve of Zastrow's guns were dismounted by noon, and the rest were silent for want of ammunition. At length at four o'clock the British Guards and the Highlanders arrived; and twelve German field-pieces attached to Granby's corps came also into action. The French likewise brought up reinforcements and the combat became livelier than ever. So far the reliefs for the garrison in the redoubt had marched down in regular order, but the fire of the French artillery was now so terrible that the men were ordered to creep down singly and dispersed, as best they could. British Guards replaced Hanoverians, and Hessians replaced British Guards; regiment after regiment taking its turn to send men to certain destruction. So the fight wore on till the dusk lowered down and the flashes of the guns turned from yellow to orange and from orange to red. The Hessians piled up the corpses of the dead into a rampart and fired on, for the redoubt though untenable must be held at any cost.

At seven o'clock the French by a desperate effort carried the passage of the bridge and fought their way close up to the redoubt, but they were met by the same dogged resistance and repulsed; and at eight o'clock, after fourteen hours of severe fighting, they abandoned the attack. Zastrow's and Granby's corps bivouacked about the bridge, and Ferdinand took up his quarters in the mill; but on the next day, none the less, the French after several unsuccessful assaults forced the garrison of Amöneberg to an honourable capitulation.

The loss of the Allies in this action was about seven hundred and fifty killed and wounded, more than a third of whom were British; the Scots Guards suffering more heavily than any corps of the troops engaged. The loss of the French rose to twelve hundred men, and the failure of their attack decided the fate of Hesse. Ferdinand, who on his advance southward had left behind a force to blockade Cassel, was able within three weeks to spare troops enough for a regular siege. On the 16th of October the trenches were opened, and on the 1st of November the town surrendered. A few days later came the news that preliminaries of a treaty had been signed. For despite all the successes of the year nothing could deter Bute from his resolution to make peace; and, indeed, knowledge of this fact had latterly made English commanders negligent and British troops backward in the field.[9] So with the fall of Cassel the war came to an end.

The terms, including as they did the cession by the French of India, except Pondicherry and Chandernagore, of French America, Canada,

9. E.g. Westphalen, vi. 885, 886. He gives other instances also.

Tobago, Dominica and St. Vincent, might not seem unfavourable to England. But it was reasonably thought at the time that Goree and Martinique should have been added, though Bute was in such haste to bring the war to an end that it was only as an afterthought that he exacted the cession of Florida by Spain in exchange for Havanna. But the true blot on the treaty was the desertion of Frederick the Great and the conclusion of a separate peace, an exhibition of selfishness and folly which recalled the Peace of Utrecht. Nevertheless Frederick was able to insist on the conditions from which he had from the first resolved not to recede, namely the retention of all that he had taken from Austria in Silesia. In February 1763 the peace was finally concluded, and Frederick entered Berlin with Ferdinand of Brunswick, who had through five campaigns guarded his right flank, appropriately seated at his right side.

The story of the war in Germany should not be closed without some few words as to Ferdinand, who, little though we know of him, was the greatest commander that led British troops to victory in Europe between Marlborough and Wellington. It was no small feat to have fought through five campaigns successfully, always with one army against two, and with at most four men against five. It is true that the conception of his most skilful movements may often be traced to Westphalen, the chief of his staff; but it is not every commander who knows when to take advice and how to act on it, or is so sure of the confidence of his troops that he can trust them always to make the best of it.

Moreover, he was confronted, though in a smaller degree, with many of the difficulties that afflicted Marlborough. His army was not an army of Allies, though generally so styled, but a mercenary army of German troops in the pay of England. So far he had the advantage of the great duke; but his force was compounded of several different elements, British, Hanoverians, Hessians, Brunswickers and Bückeburgers, who were divided by not a little jealousy as to their respective precedence, privileges, and superiority.

Of all of these the British gave him the most trouble. Their insular contempt for all foreigners was heightened by the knowledge that their comrades were mercenaries paid by their own nation; and they claimed the best quarters, the post of danger and the post of honour on all occasions. In one respect perhaps they did show superiority to the rest of the army, namely when actually on the field of battle; for beyond all doubt theirs is the chief credit for the success at Minden, at Warburg, at Emsdorff, at Wilhelmsthal, and in a lesser degree at Vellinghausen. In every action indeed they did well, and at Minden and Emsdorff they accomplished what probably no other troops in the army would have attempted. But there were scores of minor actions fought during these campaigns by German troops only, which could be matched against any other of their achievements; and there were grave defects which marred not a little the general efficiency of the British.

In the first place there was a large number of British officers of all ranks from the general to the ensign who, though brave enough, knew nothing of their duty. In the second, as Turenne had noticed a century earlier in Flanders, they were extremely negligent in the matter of outposts, patrols, and guards, owing partly to inexperience, partly to their more luxurious life at home, and partly to the contempt of danger and the spirit of gambling which is so strong in the race. Frequently Ferdinand, though quite alive to the valour of British troops in action, dared not trust them as advanced parties; whereupon the red-coats themselves, quite confident of their own sufficiency, grumbled because the foremost place was not given to them. Such jealousies as these gave endless trouble; and the disposition of the various corps, particularly of Granby's division of the Guards and Blues, required careful study as a matter not of military exigency but of policy and tact, lest the various nationalities in the army should fall at variance and take to fighting among themselves. Lastly, the British soldiers, taken as a whole, were men of inferior character to the Germans and of less experience in war; and by loose behaviour in quarters and on the march they set a bad example, which came ill from the men that looked down on all the rest of the army.

Such were the troubles which hampered Ferdinand and his staff at every turn; yet under his guidance the machine worked always with the least possible friction and the greatest development of power. He was in fact not only a great soldier but a great governor and leader of men. He combined patience, tact, and self-control with a genial and hearty courtesy, he had the faculty of selecting good men for his instruments, and above all he worked without fear or favour in noble singleness of purpose for the common cause. Of his merits as a general his campaigns speak sufficiently; and it is only necessary to add that their history was thought worthy of official study and compilation fifty years ago by the Prussian General Staff. British troops may feel proud to have so served under so able a soldier and so great and gallant a man in the campaigns which they fought in Germany for the conquest of their own empire.

CHAPTER 12

The Forge of Empire

I have followed with little interruption the long tale of hostilities which opened with the declaration of war with Spain and closed with the Peace of Fontainebleau; for despite the brief truce made by the Peace of Aix-la-Chapelle, the armies of England and France were eternally in collision either in the far east or the far west, so that to all intent the struggle resolved itself into one long war. Little though she knew it, England, when she entered wantonly and with a light heart upon the attack on the Spanish Main, had really set herself to wrestle with the French for the empire of the world. For nearly seventeen years she waited for the man who would carry her victorious through the contest; and at last he appeared. The instant change which came over the spirit of the nation when he assumed command has already been shown in the narrative of the operations. It remains only to study more closely the conduct of the war in the departments at home, and to trace the progress, not only in the organisation and training of the various branches of the army, but also in the general administration.

The war with Spain opened, as will be remembered, while the nation had not yet ceased to rail at the iniquity of a standing army, when the ascendency of the civilian element at the War Office was overpowering, and when the attitude of the ordinary citizen towards the soldier was unfriendly even to aggression. These evils, as may be guessed, did not pass away at once, even though the obnoxious red -coats were embarked or embarking for foreign service. In 1741 there was a general refusal of innkeepers to supply soldiers with food and forage, owing to the dearth caused by a winter of extraordinary severity. Such refusal was not unreasonable; and it was proposed to meet the difficulty by a new clause in the Mutiny Act.

It will hardly be believed that one member of the House of Commons made this suggestion a pretext for urging that the Mutiny Act should be dispensed with altogether, his argument being that if the system of billets should break down it would be necessary to build barracks, which would result in the subjection of the country to military government.[1] Two years later again [2] advantage was taken of an address to the king respecting his hired Hessian troops, to insert words, designed evidently for purposes of insult only, referring to, the burthensome and useless army at home. Nor did such amenities end even after the warning of 1745, for the Peace of Aix-la-Chapelle, which left the air still electric with war, was no sooner signed than the old foolish arguments against a standing army reappeared in the House of Lords, propped by such stable epigrams as "To a free state an army is like drams to a constitution."

Yet the full measure of the intoxicant which was distilled for the ruin of the nation was a niggardly draught of nineteen thousand men. These childish outbursts continued until 1754, when they ceased, at any rate until the close of the war, having served their mischievous purpose in keeping alive old animosities which common patriotism and common sense would have buried without ceremony. The ill-will of publicans and of municipalities continued likewise unabated for a few years,[3] but rapidly dwindled away before more generous feelings; and unreasonable complaints from this quarter almost disappear from the correspondence of the War Office after Dettingen.

The War Office itself was slower to mend its ways. The Secretary-at-War was quite equal to such petty jobbery as procuring the promotion of sergeants and corporals; but for all other purposes the Office showed itself at first to be utterly and hopelessly inefficient. Glimpses of maladministration have already been seen in the account of the expedition to Carthagena; but the blindness and ignorance of the officials became still more patent when Lord Stair's force was despatched to the Netherlands. The Office had not been at the pains to keep even its records in order. Not a soul seems to have known what were the rules as to allowances for forage, baggage, and the like, for troops embarking on active service; and the officials were obliged to apply to old officers who had served with Marlborough to gather precedents on such purely departmental matters as these.[4] From such beginnings it is

1. *Parl. History*, Feb. 1741.

2. *Commons Journals*, 17th Feb. 1743.

3. *E.g. Miscellaneous Orders*, 21st March 1742.

4. *Secretary's Common Letter Book*, 16th Aug., 10th Sept. 1742.

not difficult to judge of that which must have come after.

The Office of Ordnance also was at the outset as badly disorganised as the War Office. Its shortcomings have already been shown in the matter of the train sent out to Carthagena; but even a year after the departure of Cathcart it seems to have made no improvement. Transports destined for the West Indies in 1741 were obliged to put in at Cork because the water shipped at Spithead was undrinkable, and the provisions supplied for the men unfit to eat.[5] Stair, again, was despatched to the Netherlands without artillery or engineers, a deficiency which brought his force into immense contempt with the French; and when he asked for siege-guns he found that all England could afford him was but twenty twenty-four pounders[6] Small arms again were so scarce that, when the king rearmed the infantry, it was necessary to purchase ten thousand muskets and bayonets abroad.[6]

In Scotland again the inquiries of Hawley and Handasyde revealed not less flagrant neglect.[7] But this was by no means all. The general condition of the national defences both at home and abroad was most alarming; and the result was that at the opening of 1743 there was a regular panic among all the seaports, great and small, on the coast of England. Frantic applications poured into the Office of Ordnance for guns, carriages, and ammunition. It seems to have been the custom for the minor ports to erect batteries at their own expense, and to apply to the government for their armament; so that the blame for these shortcomings must rest in part upon local authorities. But there is no such excuse for carelessness in respect of regular strongholds, such as Pendennis Castle, where forty -six guns were found to be in charge of a master-gunner ninety years of age, aided by a single assistant. It was not until 1756, when ministers should have been looking after Minorca, that the Government suddenly took the alarm and threw up lines of defence at Chatham, Portsea, and Plymouth Dock.[8]

---

5. The pease after five hours of boiling were still hard, and the pieces of beef that should have weighed four pounds and served as a ration for six men weighed but eighteen ounces. *Secretary's Common Letter Book*, 7th Oct. 1741.

6. *Warrant Books*, 30th July 1741. More muskets were purchased abroad in 1750. *Ibia.* 26th Sept. 1750.

7. *Antea.*

8. *Warrant Books*, vol. lvii. Jan.-April 1743. This system of local effort has a certain interest for the present, since Newcastle was one of the ports that applied for guns. *Ibid.* vol. lviii. In the island of Jersey there were "parish-guns" kept in the parish churches, twenty-two of them in all, field-pieces. *Ibia.* vol. lxiii. For the fortification of the dockyards, see *Warrant Books*, 12th April 1756.

Colonial stations, for which the British Government was responsible, were in little better order. Newfoundland was in a deplorable condition,[9] and Gibraltar even worse; nor could all the representations of officers procure attention for them. As late as in May 1757, even after the actual fall of Minorca, Governor Lord Tyrawley wrote furiously of the state of affairs at the Rock. There had been total stagnation for many years; letters had not been answered; requests often repeated had remained unheeded.

The guns mounted on the fortress were too short, the spare carriages were too few, the palisades better fitted for hen-coops than for fortifications; in fact the defences were reduced to dangerous weakness by years of systematic neglect.[10] At St. Kitts, again, the Thirty-Eighth Foot, which for years had formed the standing garrison, was in a miserable condition; not forty *per cent* of the men were fit for service; their clothing was in rags; they had neither hats nor shoes nor cartridge-boxes nor swords.[11] Nor were the self-governing colonies more careful than the mother country. Wealthy West Indian Islands, notwithstanding the incessant warnings of their governors, found themselves at the outbreak of the war in dangerous want of arms and ammunition; and there was a rush of all the colonies both in the West Indies and in America for guns and stores, which ought to have been ready in their own magazines.[12] British carelessness, aggravated by the evil example of factious politicians in the mother country, and by the spectacle of such a creature as Newcastle in high place, had well-nigh stripped the empire of its defences.

As to the army itself, enough has been said in the account of the operations to show how unstable, despite the abundance of individual heroism, were the foundations upon which it rested. The interference of civilian administrators and of irresponsible politicians with military discipline had wrought mischief untold. Officers could not be brought to do duty with their regiments. Stair found the difficulty insuperable; so also did Hawley; so even did Cumberland in Scotland; while in the garrison of Minorca the evil transcended all bounds. Thus both the personnel and *matériel* of the army were nearly ruined, the former by persistent jobbery and meddling on the part of civil officials, the latter by the equally persistent carping of factious critics in the House of

---

9. *Warrant Books*, 9th Oct. 1746.

10. *Warrant Books*, 14th May 1757.

11. *Secretary's Common Letter Book*, 20th May 1745.

12. *Warrant Books*, vol. lvii. *passim*.

Commons, which forbade the presentation of estimates for necessary works. The military system was in fact a chaos; and it was only by the strenuous efforts of two men, who strangely enough abominated each other, that this chaos was reduced to order.

The first of these two was Cumberland. Though in many respects a martinet of a narrow type, and no great commander in the field, Cumberland was an able man, a strong man, and an administrator. He it was who first took the army seriously in hand and set himself to reduce it to discipline. He began during his first campaign by teaching the officers that they must obey. Hitherto it seems that they had taken the field as if they were going to a picnic, after the fashion of the French, travelling comfortably if not luxuriously, and neglecting all duties except that of displaying gallantry in action. Cumberland quickly put a stop to this.

The number of wheeled carriages, even for general officers, was strictly limited, and two only, one for the colonel and one for the sutler, were allowed in each regiment; while in order to reduce baggage still further, it was ordered that no officer under the rank of brigadier-general should appear either in camp or in quarters, on or off duty, except in his regimental coat, old or new.[13] Such orders may appear ludicrous at the present day, but they point to a tightening of the reins of discipline that was very sorely needed. Cumberland, too, was impatient of useless officers. He disliked the system of purchase [14] and chafed at the retention of old colonels, some so unfit for duty as to be confined in a mad-house, whose permanent presence on the active list prevented the advancement of deserving officers. His own selections were not always fortunate, as witness Hawley and Braddock, but he was fully alive to the merit of such men as Ligonier, Wolfe, and Conway, to whom, though not of his school, he gladly gave promotion.

But it is after the close of the first war, when the duke had returned to be commander-in-chief in time of peace, that his work is seen to greatest advantage. The whole tone of the War Office is changed. The Secretary-at-War almost reverts to his old position of clerk to the commander-in-chief. Military authority is predominant in military matters, and "Secretary-at-War's leave of absence" becomes a thing of the past. The functionary, who not many years before was ready to perpetrate a job for any officer with vote or interest, suddenly develops virtuous scruples and objects to the once familiar phrase, as he

13. Orders issued at Vilvorde, Oct. 10th-21st, 1745. *Miscellaneous Orders*, under date.
14. *Secretary's Common Letter Book*, 4th Oct. 1754.

never grants leave without the king's signature.[15]

But it is less by isolated examples, such as this, than by a general alteration in the methods of transacting business, that the duke's hand may be traced. There is no longer the indiscriminate correspondence with every rank of officer; but due regard is paid to the rights of superior officers as channels of communication and discipline, and to the authority of the commander-in-chief as the supreme motive power. In fact, a work of great and beneficial reform is seen to accomplish itself imperceptibly through the will and influence of a single strong man; and Cumberland's services herein have never received the recognition that they deserve. The duke, indeed, with all his foibles and prejudices was no ordinary man; and it is no surprise to one who has followed his administrative work to find that Horace Walpole ranked him with his father. Sir Robert Walpole, with Granville, Mansfield, and Pitt as one of the five great men that he had known. It is no disparagement of other members of the Royal Family to say that he was the ablest man which it has produced during the two centuries of its reign in England.

The other man who raised the tone of the army beyond estimation was of course Pitt. His share in the work, however, was very different in its nature from Cumberland's; though, without the preliminary reforms of Cumberland, his influence could hardly have been so successful as it was. Pitt's instincts respecting military administration, as distinct from the statesman's choice of a theatre of war, were thoroughly sound. He was for allowing officers to do their work, and for backing them loyally as they did it. Thus when in 1750 George Townsend, afterwards Wolfe's brigadier, proposed a clause in the Mutiny Bill to prevent non-commissioned officers or privates from being punished except by sentence of court-martial, Pitt crushed him with words which deserve to be remembered, he said:

> We have no business with the conduct of the army, nor with their complaints one against another. If we give ear to any such complaint we shall either destroy all discipline, or the House will be despised of officers and detested of soldiers.

Cumberland himself would have asked for no severer criticism than this; and yet Pitt, though perhaps unconsciously, was probably more obnoxious in his military even than in his political views to Cumberland. The duke, as has been repeatedly illustrated, was a soldier

---

15. *Secretary's Common Letter Book*, 10th August 1749.

of the rigidest German type. To use Walpole's happy phrase:

> He was as angry at an officer's infringing the minutest precept of the military rubric as at his deserting his post, and was as intent on establishing the form of spatterdashes and cockades as on taking a town or securing an advantageous situation.

In other words, he lacked that sense of proportion in matters of discipline which distinguishes the disciplinarian from the martinet. Now, despite the influence of Cumberland, there was growing up in the army a school of officers quite as strict as he was in needful matters of discipline, but less rigid, less narrow, and more humane—officers who looked upon their men not as marionettes to be dressed and undressed, used up and thrown away, but as human flesh and blood, with good feelings that could be played on, good understandings that could be instructed, self-respect that needed only to be cultivated, and high instincts that waited only to be evoked.

By giving scope to this new stamp of officer Pitt rendered the army signal service, apart from the spirit which he infused into it, as into every body of Englishmen, of energy and adventure. He was too good a master for men to be willing to return to him, unless they had fulfilled their mission or exhausted every effort to fulfil it. It is possible even that the raids on the French coast, which are a blot on his fame as a minister of war, might have been more successful (though they could never have been profitable) could he have appointed commanders of his own choice. But in truth the work of Pitt as a designer of campaigns and operations of war was by no means flawless. He had skill in thinking out how a body of men could be passed rapidly on from enterprise to enterprise.

The arrangements for the hospitals in Germany were so deficient that few of the invalids of the campaign of 1760 ever rejoined their regiments.[17] Hodgson, again, before starting for Belleisle, complained bitterly of his want of officers and of the inadequacy of the preparations made by the Office of Ordnance. These abuses were, it is true, due to the shortcomings of departments only, and therefore must not be charged against a minister who bore the burden, not only of the direction of the war, but of foreign affairs also on his shoulders; but it is, I think, a reproach to Pitt's military administration that he did not appreciate the importance of husbanding the lives of his troops. The British soldier, to put the matter in its least sentimental and most

---

17. *Secretary's Common Letter Book*, 8th and 10th Jan. 1761.

brutally practical light, has always been a most expensive article; no prodigality can be more ruinous than the careless squandering of his life, no economy so false as the grudging of his comfort.

But this failing in Pitt, serious though it be, is far outweighed by the profound policy which converted the militia into an efficient force for defence against invasion, thus liberating the regular army for purposes of conquest; and by the military insight which kept King Frederick subsidised, and Prince Ferdinand's army afoot as auxiliary to Frederick, thus turning the whole war in Europe into a diversion in England's favour. Nor was this policy wholly selfish, for loudly though the Prussians still complain of the withdrawal of Pitt's subsidies by Bute, Pitt remained in office long enough to tide Frederick over the deadliest of his peril, and so to establish the corner-stone of the present German Empire. Yet even these achievements pale before the mighty genius and the lofty enthusiasm which called the English-speaking people to arms on both sides the Atlantic to wrest from France the possession of the world. The minister of war is swallowed up in the statesman of the Empire.

The next subject of inquiry is the manner of raising that army, large beyond precedent in English history, which was accumulated by the end of the war. It will be remembered that the regiments of cavalry rose to thirty-two, and that in the infantry of the Line the numbered regiments were one hundred and twenty-four, besides two corps of Highlanders (which for some reason were known by titles of a different kind) and the brigade of Guards, making altogether a total little short of one hundred and fifty battalions. To provide recruits for such a force on the ordinary terms was impossible; and the struggle with France had hardly begun before recourse was made to the system of short service. In the session of 1743-44 was passed the first of a series of Recruiting Acts on the model of those which had been passed under Queen Anne.

The bounty offered to volunteers was four pounds, while parish-officers were empowered to impress unemployed men, for each of which they received a reward of one pound and the parish of three pounds. The standard for recruits was fixed at five feet five inches; and it was enacted that every volunteer or enlisted man should be entitled to his discharge at the end of three years. In the following session the Act was somewhat altered. The bounty to volunteers was abolished; the gift to the parish was reduced to two pounds; the standard was lowered by one inch, and the term of service was extended to five years. But as yet of course the real drain on the supply of Englishmen was not begun.

After the treaty of Aix-la-Chapelle an effort was made in the House of Commons to establish the principle of short service in time of peace. In February 1750 Mr. Thomas Pitt, a kinsman of the Great Commoner, brought forward a bill to enact that soldiers should henceforward be enlisted for ten years, and that the price of discharge should be fixed at three pounds. The scheme was opposed on the ground that men would always claim discharge after receiving their new clothing, and so defraud the colonel; that the country would be filled with idle vagabonds; and that the Pretender's adherents would take advantage of the measure to obtain military training, which would later be turned against England herself. One speaker, who supported the bill, thought ten years too long a term; and Colonel Henry Conway, an officer of much promise, while approving the principle contended that the bill as it stood would be useless, since no man would enlist for service in Ireland or the Colonies without a bounty, nor accept smaller bounty than the cost of his discharge.

More than one member who took part in the debate deplored the system of enlisting men for life, which by depriving them of hope made them idle and disorderly; but all agreed that the limitation of the term of service must inevitably lead to increased expense, since it would entail the need of a larger number of recruits. The expense of recruiting fell at that time of course on the officers, pay being allowed for a few fictitious men on the muster- rolls, and the proceeds turned into a recruiting fund. While this practice lasted, it was futile to speak of enlisting more recruits, for the officers simply could not afford it. It was useless to urge, as Conway and Oglethorpe did, that the expense of recruiting at ordinary times should be borne not by the regiment but by the public; for this would have meant an augmentation in the military estimates which was not to be thought of for a moment. So after a useful debate the bill was defeated by one hundred and fifty-four to ninety-two.[18]

On the renewal of the war a Recruiting Act identical with that of 1744-45 was passed; but in the following year (1756-57) a bounty of three pounds was again offered to volunteers, who were also allowed to take service for three years only. With this latter act the measures sanctioned by Parliament came to an end, and though this particular enactment was passed, as usual, for one year only, I conceive that it

---

18. *Parl. History*, Feb. 1750.

must have been renewed annually to the close of the war.[19] There were of course the usual abuses in the enforcement of these Acts, abuses which rose to a grave height towards the end of the war. The country was so much exhausted in 1762 that the standard was reduced to five feet two inches,[20] by which time men made a regular living by hanging about the recruiting officers, ready to accompany them before a justice and to swear that some hapless creature had taken the king's bounty.[21] Practically there was impressment for the army as for the navy; and indeed as early as in 1744 the newspapers speak openly of a general press made in Southwark for the army and marines, with the satisfactory result of a haul of two hundred men.[22]

It should be remembered, meanwhile, that since the Highlands had been thrown open, the old recruiting grounds had been considerably enlarged, and that the prospect of bearing arms had attracted great numbers of Highlanders to the ranks. Exclusive of the Forty-Second there were at least a dozen Highland battalions on the list in 1762. But to what other shifts the government may have resorted I have unfortunately been unable to discover. It is more than probable that several corps were formed under peculiar conditions of service. At least one whole regiment of Highlanders, the Duke of Sutherland's, was raised explicitly for three years only or till the close of the war;[23] and the same principle was doubtless extended to other cases. Private enterprise also came to the help of the country.

Very early in the war a society was formed in London to promote the enlistment of marines; and after Minden the Common Council of London opened subscriptions to encourage recruiting, and promised to admit men so enlisted to trade within the city forthwith, if discharged with a good character on the close of the war.[24] Then again there were regiments like Hale's and Granby's Light Dragoons which were raised by patriotic officers without cost to the country; and it is probable that these were not solitary examples. Similar advantages of economy seem to have dictated the creation in 1760 and the following years of innumerable independent companies, which after a few

19. An Order in Council of 11th July 1759 directs that men shall be enlisted for three years and for service within the kingdom only, so it is possible that the Government fell back simply on the latent power of the Crown.
20. *Secretary's Common Letter Book,* 7th Jan. 1762.
21. *Lloyd's Evening Post,* 26th Feb. 1762.
22. *London Morning Advertiser,* 18th April 1744.
23. *Miscellaneous Orders,* 7th August 1759.
24. *Gazette,* 18th August 1759.

months of isolated existence were sorted together into regiments.

The history of this system is exceedingly obscure, but it appears to have amounted practically to the offer of a commission to every man who could or would raise a hundred recruits. It was adopted amid considerable difference of opinion, and was not a success, the men so enlisted being generally unfit to carry a musket.[25] Speaking broadly, it may be asserted that during this war the ranks were filled by compulsion far more than by attraction, and by compulsion so ruthless that recruits would resort to self-mutilation to escape service.

An interesting experiment in the inner organisation of the recruiting service was instituted by advice of Lord Stair, namely the formation of two extra companies of infantry and one extra troop of cavalry for all regiments on active service. The object was to maintain a depot at home to refill all vacancies in the ranks abroad, and so to obviate the necessity of sending back recruiting officers from abroad to England. The plan did not at first commend itself to the king, and Stair was obliged to urge it repeatedly before he could obtain for it a trial; but the suggestion seems to have been approved by Cumberland, and to have been put into practice for a time, though the additional companies were presently amalgamated into distinct regiments. Therewith the whole system of the feeding of regiments abroad fell back on the old plan of drafting; and during the Seven Years' War regiments at home, particularly the dragoons,[26] were raised to a considerable strength to serve simply as recruiting depots for regiments abroad. From a regimental standpoint the story of the war is one of drafting, drafting, drafting, with of course all the vices that had been condemned by Marlborough attendant on the practice. The garrisons of captured places suffered terribly from this evil.

A medal might have increased the flow of recruits and reconciled men to service beyond the sea, not one was issued. Ferdinand of Brunswick received the Garter, but nothing was done to commemorate for lesser men the share that they had taken in the conquest of an empire.

---

25. Conway complained much of the drafts from the independent companies sent to Germany, the men being weakly, young, and undersized (*Secretary's Common Letter Book*, 2nd June 1761; and see *Correspondence of George III. with Lord North*, vol. i.). The king ascribes the system to Charles Townsend, but it was begun before he became Secretary-at-War.

26. Thus other Light Dragoons besides the Fifteenth really partook in the glory of Emsdorff; one of the officers killed being, though formerly of the Fifteenth, an officer of the Seventeenth, who probably took a draft of his new regiment with him.

I turn now to consideration of the military progress in the three combatant branches of the army. In the cavalry an early change, which has been perpetuated by certain regimental titles to the present day, was the conversion of the three senior regiments of Horse into Dragoons, with the names which they still retain of the First, Second, and Third Dragoon Guards. This was done in December 1746 and was apparently part of a general scheme of economy; for at precisely the same time the Third and Fourth troops of the Life Guards were disbanded, and two troops only reserved, together with two troops of Horse Grenadier Guards. But there seems also to have been somewhat of a craze for dragoons at the moment, first because their pay was small, and secondly, because Frederick the Great, in imitation of the Austrians, had made greater mobility the rule for all cavalry.

In truth the old distinctions between Horse and Dragoons were disappearing fast and becoming very much a question of names. The French indeed still made it a rule not to place dragoons in the line of battle; but the horse in their army was distinguished by being heavily clad in defensive armour. Ligonier, who loved the cavalry above all arms, boldly advised the disregard of all fanciful differences, and the issue of defensive armour to the British dragoons; but his recommendation remained unnoticed for twelve years, when, in a true spirit of pedantry, cuirasses and iron skull-caps were given in 1758 to the Blues and in 1760 to the Third and Fourth Horse, or to give them their present names, the Sixth and Seventh Dragoon Guards.

Another defect noted by Ligonier in the organisation of the cavalry was the extreme weakness of the British squadrons as compared with the French; for remedy of which he purposed to raise the strength of troops of horse to fifty and of dragoons to seventy-five troopers. Such a reform would have been valuable as a return to Cromwell's system of making the units strong enough to provide full employment for the officers; but the authorities settled the question in a far more simple fashion by ordaining that three troops, instead of two as heretofore, should be the strength of a squadron on service. The country has waited long for Ligonier's suggestion to be adopted, and it is only within very recent years, if now, that it has at last grasped the soundness of the principle.

More important as a step forward was the institution of Light Dragoons, begun, as has been told, by the establishment first of light troops and later of complete light regiments. The example in this case came from a corps formed during the Scottish rebellion of 1745, the

Duke of Kingston's Light Dragoons, which did so good service that, though disbanded after Culloden, it was at once reformed as the Duke of Cumberland's own. As such it distinguished itself greatly at Lauffeld, and Cumberland pleaded hard that it might be spared after the Peace of Aix-la-Chapelle; but with the usual blindness it was disbanded, and thus a regiment of quite unusual value and promise was sacrificed.

Happily the Fifteenth Light Dragoons made a most brilliant beginning for the new branch of the cavalry, and assured its success. The light dragoons were distinguished by wearing a helmet of lacquered copper or leather, and were armed with carbine, bayonet, pistol, and sword, carrying also entrenching tools in their holsters. Their horses are described as of the nag or hunter kind, standing from fourteen hands three inches to fifteen hands one inch; and their saddlery was lighter than that of the ordinary dragoon. Being intended for employment as irregular troops they were known from the first in England as hussars; but though they received special training in horsemanship and in firing, even at a gallop, from the saddle, they had little or no instruction in the duties of reconnaissance, which were the peculiar function of the hussar. Nothing could be more characteristic of the difference between the true and the false light cavalry than the behaviour of the Fifteenth at Emsdorff, who charged through and through the French infantry without hesitation, while the Prussian hussars, never coming to close quarters, lost not a man nor a horse. Fortunately it was not the true hussar that was most sorely needed on that day.

For the rest, before the opening of the war the old system of manoeuvre by turning every horse in his own ground had given place to that by wheeling of small divisions, although the ranks were still formed three deep. It does not appear that the drill introduced by Frederick the Great for field-movements was adopted either in whole or in part, though possibly it may have been practised by individual colonels. Shock action our cavalry did not need to learn from Frederick, having learned it already of Marlborough; but our squadrons seem as usual to have been prone to their besetting sin of unwillingness to rally after a successful charge. It was this wild galloping forward that wrecked Ligonier's heroic regiments at Lauffeld.

On the other hand, Granby's squadrons, for all their leader's impetuosity, seem to have been well in hand at Warburg, and to have done their work with spirit and yet subject to control. But a trot of two hours before coming into action had probably rubbed the keen edge off both horses and men.

Passing next to the artillery we approach the most remarkable development observable during this period in the whole army. The gunners after 1741 are found to raise the reputation of their corps steadily in all parts of the world. Their place as yet was still on the left of the line, yielding precedence to the whole of the rest of the army, but they were entitling themselves to a higher station. At first the gunners are seen at work principally with the battalion guns, light three-pounders or six-pounders, which though attached to the infantry were served by artillerymen. [27] In Germany, however, we find the guns before Minden scientifically concentrated and handled in large masses by the skill of the Count of Lippe Bückeburg; and there the British batteries win the admiration of the most critical artillerists in Europe, and their officers the special praise of Ferdinand of Brunswick himself.

The influence of the academy had told early; but it is a still more significant fact that British Artillery officers, not obtaining their commissions by purchase, did not rise to command without knowledge of their work. The variety of guns issued for the field was very great, and though three-pounders seem to have given place in the Seven Years' War to light six-pounders as the lightest ordnance employed, yet there were also heavy six-pounders, light and heavy twelve-pounders, howitzers and twenty-four pounders. It was probably the light six-pounders that amazed the whole army at Warburg by advancing at the gallop, a feat which was the more remarkable since drivers and horses were still hired, and not part and parcel of the corps as at present.[28] Finally, Mauvillon bears witness that the British guns were kept far the cleanest and in the most perfect order of any in the whole Allied army.

Of the Engineers it is impossible to speak as favourably; indeed it is almost an extreme assumption to assert their existence except in name. Stair had not even one efficient engineer in the Low Countries, and was obliged to engage Dutch and Austrian officers, while Hodgson at Belleisle was inefficient. The fact is less remarkable when it is remembered that the sea obviates the necessity for the fortification of inland towns in England. In truth the French engineers, in respect both of the skill of the officers and the organisation of the men, seem to have stood far above the rest of Europe, while the British probably

---

27. Two guns was the allowance for a battalion, and the detachment to serve them consisted of an officer, two non-commissioned officers, and 12 men. *Warrant Books,* 30th June 1758.

28. The three-pounders were mounted on two-wheeled "galloping carriages," drawn by three horses; the six-pounders required four if not five horses.

stood lowest of all.

Lastly we come to the Infantry. The great characteristic of the British infantry throughout the war is the excellence of their fire-discipline and the deadly accuracy of their fire. It is curious, therefore, to read in the most popular military handbook of the time that it was precisely in the matter of fire-discipline that the British were reckoned defective, so defective that they were accounted inferior to the Dutch and were obliged to comfort themselves with the reflection that the Dutch were naturally more phlegmatic of temperament. The author is careful to point out that Dutch superiority lay in discipline only, so it is reasonable to infer that the British improved rapidly in this respect during the war. And such indeed is the conclusion to be drawn from the study of the various actions.

At Dettingen the fire though deadly was unsteady; at Fontenoy it was nearly perfect; at Minden, where the British stood motionless until the French cavalry was within ten paces, it was quite admirable. It is commonly supposed that this improvement was due to the adoption of Prussian methods, but I can find no ground for the assumption. The Prussian manual and firing exercise did indeed find its way to the First Guards in 1756; and there still exists record of a petition from some aged pensioners against the cruelty of an ensign who drilled them every day through the winter in the Prussian exercise, though they had hardly clothes to cover their nakedness; but this has no bearing on the action of Fontenoy in 1745.

The truth is that in the matter of attack the British had nothing to learn from the Prussians, either in the cavalry or the infantry. Marlborough had taught them the superiority of shock-action and platoon-fire long before Frederick the Great was born; and all that the Prussian school had to teach, apart from this and from the discipline which went to its perfect execution, was the precision of march learned from pendulum and pace-stick, and certain undeniable improvements in the manoeuvre of a regiment or battalion. It has been suggested, (Carlyle), indeed, that a Prussian column at Fontenoy might have manoeuvred its way to victory by sheer perfection of drill and discipline; but this begs the question whether they would have preserved their order as admirably as the British during the advance. Certainly it is hardly conceivable that even Prussian regiments could have behaved more perfectly under very heavy fire and in the presence of an overwhelming force of cavalry than the six British battalions at Minden.

But the most important changes in the infantry were akin to those in the cavalry. The first was the practice of massing the grenadiers of the army into battalions, which though forbidden by the king as an Austrian innovation when first proposed by Stair, was ultimately adopted both in America and in Germany. The next was the introduction of light troops for the work of skirmishing and for such rapid movements and special duties as were committed in the cavalry to hussars. In the British Army the first representatives of this class of infantry were the Highlanders, who for this reason were armed with short muskets or carbines and were drawn up outside the line in the formal order of battle. Stair had begged for Highlanders in their native dress as early as in 1742, and to his influence probably was due their presence at Fontenoy.

During the Seven Years' War, as has been seen, they were employed in every quarter of the globe and did excellent service.

In truth, though there were lessons which the British might learn with profit from foreign nations, both as to what they should imitate and what they should avoid, the best of their instruction was that which they gained from their own hard experience in lands remote from Europe. The influence of King Frederick the Great was perverted in great measure for ill to the army. The king and Cumberland had both of them a passion for minute details of dress, facings, lace, buttons, cockades, and the like, and were dear lovers of the tight clothing and inelasticity of movement which characterised the Prussian school. There can be no doubt, on the other hand, that strict insistence on cleanliness and smartness is indispensable, and that correctness and uniformity of dress are valuable aids to discipline and to *esprit de corps*.

Such little distinctions as that the coats of Horse should be lapelled to the skirt and of Dragoons to the waist, while those of Light Dragoons should be without lapels of any kind, are harmless in themselves, and give men a pride and an interest in their branch of the service; but the powdering of hair, the docking of the old-fashioned serviceable coats, and the straitening of every article of raiment were no gain to efficiency, no improvement to health, and in the eyes of Englishmen, at first, no embellishment as to appearance. Had the king turned his thoughts to diminishing the weight on a soldier's back, or devising suitable equipment for tropical climates, he might have saved lives untold; but many years were still to elapse before such simple matters as these were to receive due notice.

The beautiful accuracy of drill enjoined by Frederick was turned to good account by the British on many fields in Europe and in India;

but his excellent discipline on active service both on and off duty was by no means so faithfully copied, as Ferdinand of Brunswick found out to his cost, (Mauvillon). Yet at any rate the British had an example of the worst that they must eschew in the armies of the French. Therein:

There was no discipline, no subordination, no order on the march, in the camp or even in the battlefield. The very subalterns had their mistresses with them, and officers often left their men to accompany them on the march in their carriages. Everything that could contribute to the luxury of the officers was found in the French camp. At one time there were twelve thousand waggons accompanying Soubise's army which belonged to sutlers and shopkeepers, though the army was not fifty thousand strong. . . . Balls were given in camp and officers often left their posts to dance a minuet. They laughed at the orders of their leaders and only obeyed when it suited them.— (Archenholz)

From such folly and disgrace as this Cumberland's attachment to the stricter models of Germany delivered the army.

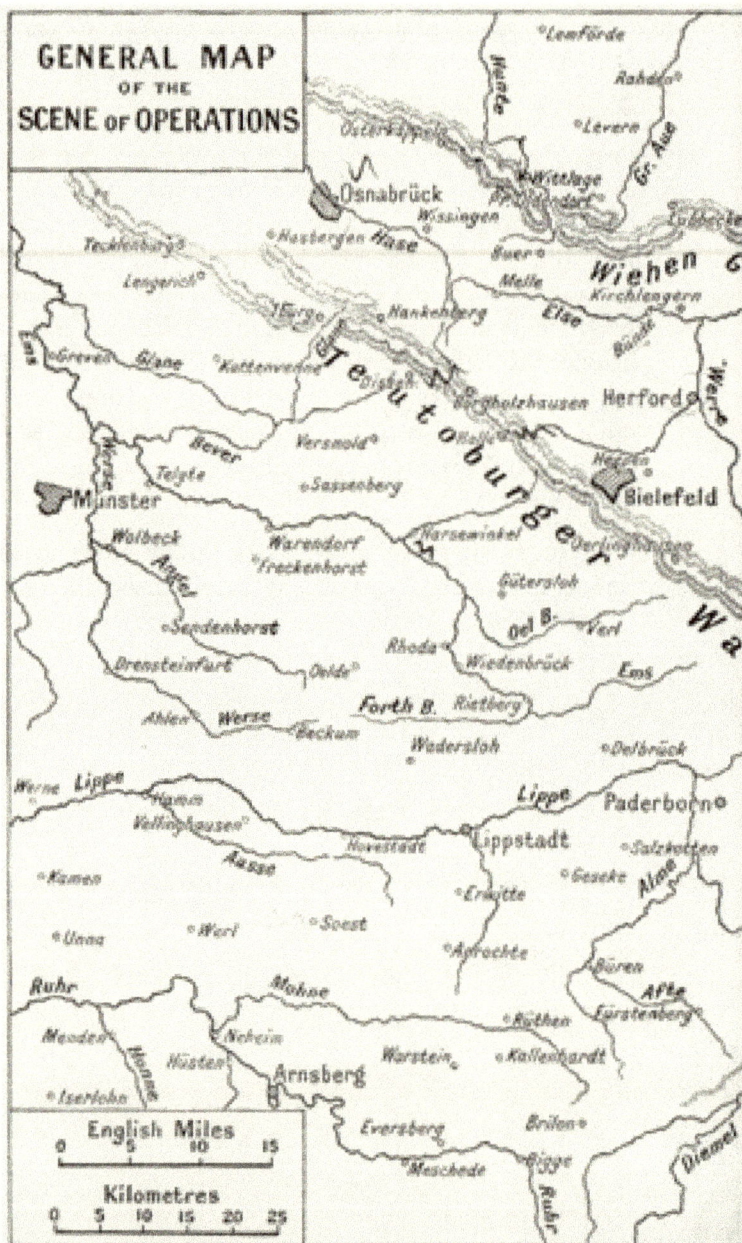

GENERAL MAP
OF THE
SCENE OF OPERATIONS

English Miles
0   5   10   15

Kilometres
0   5   10   15   20   25

LEONAUR

ALSO FROM LEONAUR
AVAILABLE IN SOFTCOVER OR HARDCOVER WITH DUST JACKET

ESCAPE FROM THE FRENCH *by Edward Boys*—A Young Royal Navy Midshipman's Adventures During the Napoleonic War.

THE VOYAGE OF H.M.S. PANDORA *by Edward Edwards R. N. & George Hamilton, edited by Basil Thomson*—In Pursuit of the Mutineers of the Bounty in the South Seas—1790-1791.

MEDUSA *by J. B. Henry Savigny and Alexander Correard and Charlotte-Adélaïde Dard* —Narrative of a Voyage to Senegal in 1816 & The Sufferings of the Picard Family After the Shipwreck of the Medusa.

THE SEA WAR OF 1812 VOLUME 1 *by A. T. Mahan*—A History of the Maritime Conflict.

THE SEA WAR OF 1812 VOLUME 2 *by A. T. Mahan*—A History of the Maritime Conflict.

WETHERELL OF H. M. S. HUSSAR *by John Wetherell*—The Recollections of an Ordinary Seaman of the Royal Navy During the Napoleonic Wars.

THE NAVAL BRIGADE IN NATAL *by C. R. N. Burne*—With the Guns of H. M. S. Terrible & H. M. S. Tartar during the Boer War 1899-1900.

THE VOYAGE OF H. M. S. BOUNTY *by William Bligh*—The True Story of an 18th Century Voyage of Exploration and Mutiny.

SHIPWRECK! *by William Gilly*—The Royal Navy's Disasters at Sea 1793-1849.

KING'S CUTTERS AND SMUGGLERS: 1700-1855 *by E. Keble Chatterton*—A unique period of maritime history-from the beginning of the eighteenth to the middle of the nineteenth century when British seamen risked all to smuggle valuable goods from wool to tea and spirits from and to the Continent.

CONFEDERATE BLOCKADE RUNNER *by John Wilkinson*—The Personal Recollections of an Officer of the Confederate Navy.

NAVAL BATTLES OF THE NAPOLEONIC WARS *by W. H. Fitchett*—Cape St. Vincent, the Nile, Cadiz, Copenhagen, Trafalgar & Others.

PRISONERS OF THE RED DESERT *by R. S. Gwatkin-Williams*—The Adventures of the Crew of the Tara During the First World War.

U-BOAT WAR 1914-1918 *by James B. Connolly/Karl von Schenk*—Two Contrasting Accounts from Both Sides of the Conflict at Sea D uring the Great War.

LEONAUR

ALSO FROM LEONAUR

AVAILABLE IN SOFTCOVER OR HARDCOVER WITH DUST JACKET

THE FALL OF THE MOGHUL EMPIRE OF HINDUSTAN *by H. G. Keene*—By the beginning of the nineteenth century, as British and Indian armies under Lake and Wellesley dominated the scene, a little over half a century of conflict brought the Moghul Empire to its knees.

LADY SALE'S AFGHANISTAN *by Florentia Sale*—An Indomitable Victorian Lady's Account of the Retreat from Kabul During the First Afghan War.

THE CAMPAIGN OF MAGENTA AND SOLFERINO 1859 *by Harold Carmichael Wylly*—The Decisive Conflict for the Unification of Italy.

FRENCH'S CAVALRY CAMPAIGN *by J. G. Maydon*—A Special Correspondent's View of British Army Mounted Troops During the Boer War.

CAVALRY AT WATERLOO *by Sir Evelyn Wood*—British Mounted Troops During the Campaign of 1815.

THE SUBALTERN *by George Robert Gleig*—The Experiences of an Officer of the 85th Light Infantry During the Peninsular War.

NAPOLEON AT BAY, 1814 *by F. Loraine Petre*—The Campaigns to the Fall of the First Empire.

NAPOLEON AND THE CAMPAIGN OF 1806 *by Colonel Vachée*—The Napoleonic Method of Organisation and Command to the Battles of Jena & Auerstädt.

THE COMPLETE ADVENTURES IN THE CONNAUGHT RANGERS *by William Grattan*—The 88th Regiment during the Napoleonic Wars by a Serving Officer.

BUGLER AND OFFICER OF THE RIFLES *by William Green & Harry Smith*—With the 95th (Rifles) during the Peninsular & Waterloo Campaigns of the Napoleonic Wars.

NAPOLEONIC WAR STORIES *by Sir Arthur Quiller-Couch*—Tales of soldiers, spies, battles & sieges from the Peninsular & Waterloo campaigns.

CAPTAIN OF THE 95TH (RIFLES) *by Jonathan Leach*—An officer of Wellington's sharpshooters during the Peninsular, South of France and Waterloo campaigns of the Napoleonic wars.

RIFLEMAN COSTELLO *by Edward Costello*—The adventures of a soldier of the 95th (Rifles) in the Peninsular & Waterloo Campaigns of the Napoleonic wars.